T0198666

LIFE, DEATH,
—— AND THE ——
BIRTH
OF TRUTH

A Medium's Communication
with the Other Side

Caroline Byrd

BALBOA.
PRESS
A DIVISION OF HAY HOUSE

Balboa Press books may be ordered through
booksellers or by contacting:

Balboa Press
A Division of Hay House
1663 Liberty Drive
Bloomington, IN 47403
www.balboapress.com.au
1 (877) 407-4847

Print information available on the last page.

ISBN: 978-1-5043-0891-5 (sc)
ISBN: 978-1-5043-0892-2 (e)

Balboa Press rev. date: 07/12/2017

This book is lovingly and respectfully
dedicated to my family members, friends
and colleagues whose journey through life
and death has deeply touched my life.

CONTENTS

ACKNOWLEDGMENTS

I extend my deepest gratitude and appreciation to all those individuals who have assisted in the manifestation of this book. Especially to those who have crossed over sharing their experiences into the afterlife. I thank Kirsten Xanthopoulos for her diligent proof reading and editing. In addition; many thanks to my friends, family members, clients and students, who supported me unconditionally throughout this entire process.

PREFACE

Finally after many years and life's experiences, this book has been written. If you would have asked me twenty five years ago "are you writing a book?" I would have laughed at you, and said no way. Writing a book is what someone else does. Not something I would do.

For the past 15 years I have been streaming this book. That means writing, writing and writing, with no structure, no idea of where it was heading. I just knew I had to document my knowledge with the understanding I have reached of myself through life and death. Now I can see clearly three stages of my life. Through this book I share the first stage where I finally accept the veil between life and death. The acceptance happened over many years when facing mortality through varying stages of grief after close and personal encounters with death.

At a very young age I remember feeling scared of the bogey man, my own shadows. I never liked watching horror movies, especially where ghosts were involved. I would hide behind the pillow or close my eyes when scary scenes were on the television. Yet there was no reason why this feeling was with me. Until one day as an adult I was shown a vision in my mind of me as a 3 year old child, one night standing in the corner of my bedroom crying. I looked up and saw the door handle too far to reach. I was talking to strangers, spirits people in my room telling them to leave me alone, go away. That was the last time I recalled having these experiences.

My childhood was mediocre with 3 older sisters, loving parents who raised us the best they knew how. Through childhood I would be very expressive with my thoughts, opinions of life and people. I was always being told to think before you speak. Not understanding why, just knowing what I was saying was true. In other words I had no filter, I never looked at consequences. My inner knowing was very strong, never questioning what I knew, felt or heard. I would just speak it.

I was drawn to the occult, anything different that felt comfortable in my body. In my early teenage years I was the hippy of the family. Dressing casually, wearing oils of frank incense and sandalwood. I loved finding the hidden shops behind the mainstream streets. The feeling that I would experience in these places sat well in me. It was as though I was home, yet never really understood why. Later in my late teens I bought my first set of tarot cards. I loved looking at them, interpreting the story of the tarot. Something deep inside me was touched as I began to unravel.

My journey began as people would ask me for a reading. I was not professional at all in fact; I was so relaxed enjoying a wine while opening to the cards and the person in front of me. It was easy lots of fun moments. In my early twenties I noticed boredom creeping into my readings. I could sense, feel, see and hear so much more behind the future predictions. I couldn't contain myself and my work began as an emotional reader. I would ask people "Do you really want me to read for you?" I knew the moment I sat in front of someone the truth of life appeared as I spoke from a deep knowing within.

Finally I found a vessel that allowed me to speak truth without being told off or being attacked for. It was my safe place to express from. Over time I began to feel something was missing. I would only read for family, friends and self. Then slowly it faded as life changed.

My own emotional journey began; as my twenties were full of fear. Anger through anxiety created many ailments and hospital encounters. Marrying at 19 and having my son at 20, was a blessing for me. For it was the last time I was able to conceive due to illness. My marriage was not easy; it was very much a roller coaster ride emotionally. I would use the tarot cards often. They helped me understand myself through life. They were my greatest friend, always there when I was in need.

The knowing intuitive side of me became

heightened in my marriage as I found it difficult to relax. These heightened moments mirrored my childhood. The similarities of the child knowing deep inside that something was about to happen. When I look back I was always in some form of communication with what I would call the voice. Remembering my experience as a three year old I told Spirit to go away, they did. Well I thought they did; they just stopped appearing outside of me.

Over the years I would go to many tarot readers to get confirmation of what I was feeling. There were a few times when they gave my money back telling me; sorry I can't read for you. They shared with me; my guidance has told them I need to do this for myself. How frustrating those times were.

It all changed at the age of twenty nine. My husband died in a car accident. My inner experiences opened wide. Many times thinking I was going mad. I began to question life and death. What was real and what was my imagination. It was as though every sensory perception was in overdrive. I could see things, hear things, feel things, and just know certain things. My world was thrown into a new direction, one that I tried to ignore. The more I ignored my experiences, the stronger they became. Finally after many moments of Spirit in my home, my inner vision and my energy field, I knew I had to accept this was my reality, I can't hide from it.

I was guided to learn meditation after many moments of anxiety, it was my saving grace. The peaceful calming feelings would help to unravel what was happening to me. I began to document daily events and synchronistic moments. Through meditation I was able to ground myself in a way that helped my daily life. Reality and the unseen world merged into each other. I found myself questioning the truth of who we are, why we are here and what is life after death.

I began to understand a different perspective from my childhood beliefs of life and death. Not that I had many to refer to, I literally had no major trauma or religious upbringing to shadow what I was feeling. My parents were not religious; they were atheists. There were no bibles, church or talks in the home of God, Jesus or a Devil. During my grief, especially at times of people passing, I would feel the deep knowing from my inner guidance, which I called the voice. I was thankful for not having deep core religious beliefs. I was able to truly listen, while understanding my personal experiences, without any preconceived ideas.

It seemed death was facing me, many people passed over. With each passing I would have a deeper experience. Each one showed me another truth about life through death. I became inspired to learn more as I gained different insights from the voice and the world of spirit. My life changed for the better. Delving into myself I realised there was much more to this life than the body and what we were taught at school.

The voice within is my constant companion in this journey. I am blessed to be able to share my insights, truth and deep understanding of the Souls embodiment. It is my desire to help others to understand life through death, yet understand death in life. This subject of life and death can be hard for people to delve into, especially when it is raw through the stages of grief.

My encounter with Spirit and the other side are documented in this book. I hope those of you who read my book can have your own understanding of the experiences you may have yet not fully understood. I believe that healing can happen in an instant. It may be your time to heal as you read my words. You may gravitate to a particular chapter as you connect to the experience and the outcome of that experience.

We all have or will be touched by death at some stage on the path of life. You may be searching for a particular insight into your own encounter. My truth is my I experience; your truth is your experience. Some of these words may help you heal your own grief. My motto in life is to help others help themselves. So if this book touches just one person the job is done. My guidance, the voice and many who have gone before me will finally be heard through my writings. I hope you are one of them who heal as you read my words.

Many years ago I heard the voice share this statement with me. I now use it as a guide to life's purpose.

"When experience brings a quality to life and understanding allows a change to begin. Change that brings positive outcomes and brings you back to your natural self"

CHAPTER 1

THE UNVEILING

*This was the night my life changed;
the veil had been lifted between
the worlds of life and death*

CHAPTER 1

THE UNVEILING

It all began one winters evening in 1991 when I started to question the meaning of life and death. After a marriage break down, and an emotional roller coaster ride of mental, physical, and emotional abuse, my life was beginning to resemble some form of normality. I had suppressed many emotions as I began a new relationship. One of the hardest emotions to hide was the pain of not being with my 8-year-old son. In the beginning of this roller coaster ride as I call it, I had no idea how to heal my mind, my emotions, or how to work on myself at all. All I knew was when something hurt me or a situation overwhelmed me, I had to push it away and be strong to get on with life.

Throughout my separation, I struggled with allowing my husband to have any contact details of mine especially where I was living and my phone numbers. The rationale for this was he had not accepted the end of our marriage and was angry and emotionally abusive; not giving him my details helped me feel safe, secure, and out of his reach. For the wellbeing of our son, I would give him a family member's phone number for emergencies, or for times that my son wanted to talk to me. Totally in denial of my deeper emotional state, I continued with my life as though everything was alright.

Dreams began to feel real, as though I was living what was in my dream. I would wake up and feel an emotion, or have an ominous feeling about certain dreams. I found that I could recall dreams with ease as if they were happening right now, not a few days or weeks ago. Then one night I had a dream that felt so real, that I woke up in the middle of the night with my whole body shaking and vibrating. I dreamt I walked into a morgue and saw all steel doors on the wall that represented a body behind each one. I knew I was there to view someone but I had no idea who it was.

The man in my dream opened one of the doors and pulled out a metal slab; there was a body covered with a white sheet. I felt a surge of fear rise up through my body as I was unsure who I would see under the sheet. As he pulled back the sheet, I saw my husband lying there, so I walked toward the body to take a closer look. To my surprise, I wasn't scared, or sad, or confused, I actually felt calm; I wondered how he managed to get himself into this predicament. As I looked at his body, I noticed there were two defining marks on him; one on his face and the other on his chest. As I looked at the mark on his face, I heard a voice internally speak to me and say, "This can be from a car accident." Then I looked at the mark on his chest, and again I heard the internal voice speak to me, "This could be from a shot gun wound." I suddenly woke up in my room, in my bed, and again I heard the internal voice say to me, "It will be either a car accident or a shot gun wound." Eventually I fell back to sleep and woke in the morning and thought, wow, what a strange dream that was. Life continued, yet not a day went by without some form of emotion trying to rise to the surface, wanting to be faced.

Then one evening, I received a phone call to ring my husband. I never knew what tone the conversations would take, so I was always on guard, waiting and ready to be abused or yelled at. I dialled the number and felt the adrenalin rise in my body. When my husband answered the call, my heart jolted for a moment until he began to talk. He told me that he had been in hospital with a blow to the head from a fight, and that he was alright. I listened, but it felt strange because he was usually aggressive, yet he was calm and sort of in control. I asked him if our son was alright and he told me, "he is good and it will not be long until you have him back" I listened but didn't believe him, I replied, "yeah you have said this before, but it never happens." He kept telling me, "it's true, you will have him back soon", then continued to tell me that he would be dead soon. He kept repeating, I will be dead soon. I didn't believe him and I definitely didn't connect it to my dream, which happened a few months earlier. I spoke to my son, and the phone call ended, yet I was feeling a bit apprehensive about this call; I am usually being abused in some manner but that never happened.

Over the 10 years we were married, my husband would often talk to me about him dying young. He would say to me, "I will be dead before I am 34." I would laugh at him and reply, "yeah right, how do you know this?" and he would always say, "I just know I will be dead before I am 34."Therefore, it became something I never forgot. We had on occasions even discussed his funeral, what he wanted, how he was to be buried, and even laughing at his choice of music he wanted to play through his funeral. At these times, I never actually thought that he may know something that was so far out of any persons' control, especially his own death.

The following Saturday evening, I went to bed early after a long day at work. I fell asleep quickly and was in a deep sleep when I woke up suddenly. I looked at the clock and it was 1.11am. I felt very uncomfortable, my jaw was feeling tense, my teeth were clenched, and I felt an overwhelming agitation and anger rush through my body. I went into the lounge room and sat down, and I heard in my mind my sons name repeating over and over. Suddenly and uncontrollably I burst into tears. I was sobbing, missing my son, yet still feeling confused as to what was happening as this had never happened to me before. After about 30 minutes, my emotions settled down and I went back to bed. I must have fallen asleep again because before I knew it my phone was ringing; it was now 2.10am. I picked up the phone and heard my sister's voice; she told me a police officer needs to contact me, as my husband had been fatally injured earlier in the evening.

I dialled the number and heard a man's voice, "Hello Sergeant Dudley speaking" I heard the words and felt confused, and began to feel agitation in my body once more. My mind was racing; was this real? Did this actually happen? Maybe it was a mistake. I was in shock, my entire body was numb, but my mind kept racing; my son, where was my son? Was he safe? As I spoke to the officer, my fear became a reality. My husband had died earlier that evening in a car accident, but luckily my son was not with him; he was safe with friends. At that moment, I began to shut out the imagery and thoughts that were going through my mind. I had a mission and that was to protect my son from this tragic and emotional night.

This was the night my life changed; the veil had been lifted between the worlds of life and death. It changed in so many ways and with so many experiences that my beliefs of life and death became blurred; confusion and fear were a natural state. My husband had died and was buried 8 weeks before his 34th birthday. I was in shock at first; did he deliberately have a car accident? Did he actually mean to die? So many thoughts were racing through my mind for days and weeks, until I found out he was a passenger, and most likely asleep when the accident occurred; apparently, forensics and the police at the scene can piece it all together. That never really helped me though, because he had died when he stated he would; was he psychic? How could he have known this?

After the funeral, I began to experience strange things happening in my room at night. I began to wake up around the same time each night with a jolt, as though someone had woken me. I would look towards the same point in my room near my walk-in wardrobe, and see a silhouette of a man standing, looking at me. The more I looked the less I could see, until the image would fade away. At first, I thought my mind was playing tricks on me, but how could that be. I was frightened, yet I just knew it was my husband watching me. I started to feel panic at the thought of him being there in my room. I couldn't rationalize the truth behind this. He had died, yet somehow, he was still here in my room. I tried not to think about it too much, and once again, pushed this down; I became good at blocking my fears.

The sense of anticipation and fear continued to grip me as I would wake up and feel and see the presence in my room. I tried to ignore the feeling and not open my eyes, because seeing the image was the part that made my heart and mind race. As I lay awake with my eyes closed, I sensed a shadow pass-by my face. The presence was no longer near the wardrobe; it was now standing beside my bed. What could I do? This was out of my control. I was terrified in my own home, my own sanctuary. (I lived in The Sanctuary)

A few months later, I was still having these strange and frightening occurrences, so I decided to ask my husband to stop scaring and terrorising me. Slowly, the imagery began to stop externally, but it began in my dreams. I would be in a dream and then I would see him just standing, looking at me; he never spoke, just stared at me. One evening, I was in a lovely dream enjoying myself walking up a hill when I saw him. He was just standing, looking at me, but this time I woke up in my dream long enough to say something. I was still hurt and frightened, but now there was also anger; I yelled at him and told him to get out of my dream. I said, "This is my dream and you don't belong here." He looked at me and without saying a word; he turned away from me, walked over the hill, and disappeared. I was shocked, it actually worked, and he left my dream, and stayed out of my dreams for a long time after that.

Life started to get back to normal, going to work, settling my son into his new home and school; living just took over. Yet in the back of my mind I was always aware of the presence with me, in my home, and everywhere I went. It's as though a shadow was following me, even when it was dark.

At work one day, an elderly male customer came in to pay for some hardware, and being a cold winter's day I was behind the counter warming my hands and feet. He looked at me standing there and told me, "The man standing next to you loves you so much." I quickly looked up at him and asked, "What do you mean?" He again told me, "The man who is with you loves you so much." I froze and just stared at him. He laughed and said, "There is a man in spirit standing on your right-hand side, and he's telling me to let you know that he loves you so much." I had never seen this man before in the shop and I was a bit wary of him, so as I do, I just laughed and brushed it off and continued to serve him. He left the shop, and I was left with a feeling of confusion and fear once again. My mind started to fill with questions; how did he know? Who was he? What did he actually see? Too late, the man had disappeared.

From then on, the night time images started to come back, and I just knew in my heart that it was my husband trying to contact me. For some reason, I didn't want to believe this, I just wanted to get on with my life and forget all about these fears.

It was a few weeks later while at work, when I had another experience. An elderly male customer told me the same thing, "the man who is standing next to you loves you so much." This time I was quick to ask him, "what can you see? Why are you telling me this?" He shared with me, "the man who is with you wants you to know that his love for you is so deep, and that he needs you to know that he is sorry for the things that happened between you both." He then began to describe my husband and his description of him was exact. I had no doubt in my mind that he was seeing the spirit of my husband. This became a frequent occurrence, where strangers, out of the blue, would share with me what they were seeing and feeling around me.

Around the same time, I was at work and having a cup of tea just thinking about life, the events of life, and where I was now because of them. A song came on the radio and took my attention away from my thoughts. It was as though someone had turned up the sound of the radio at that moment. It was all I could hear, and there was no one physically in the shop. The words I heard were, "And I know you're shining down on me from heaven like so many friends we've lost along the way, and I know eventually we will be together one sweet day." One sweet day by Mariah Carey, this was huge; the whole song touched every cell in my body. I listened deeply to the words as they ran through my heart and mind, knowing this was my husband wanting me to hear this. I burst into tears and felt his presence so strongly as though he was wrapping his arms around me. The lyrics for the whole song were exactly our dynamic, how I was feeling and how he was feeling in Spirit. Once the moment and the song had finished, the radio returned to its normal low volume as a gentle background sound in the shop. This was the moment that I had to truly surrender into the truth, the truth between life and death, the truth that my husband had died in body but was present in spirit.

The movements in my room at night became more frequent. I noticed other shadows in my room, and not just the feeling and movement of my husband. Things that go bump in the night became a common theme for me, always being aware of someone or something moving in my peripheral vision. Waking up was a regular occurrence and I always expected to see someone standing beside my bed.

One evening as I slept, I was startled by a loud noise in the bedroom. I looked towards the bottom of the bed where the noise was coming from, and to my surprise, the lid of my plastic wash basket was on the floor spinning as though someone had just knocked it onto the floor. I looked around the room but couldn't see any of the usual signs that spirit was there, no shadows or strange energy movements in the atmosphere. I got out of bed and placed the lid back on the basket and thought to myself; there was definitely someone there because that lid would not have fallen off by itself. Eventually I fell back to sleep and woke the next morning feeling perplexed as to what had happened that night. Around lunchtime, I heard news from my dad that my great aunt had died. I instantly knew it was her in my bedroom the previous night. I asked my Dad, "when did she die?" and he replied, "it must have been sometime through the night, we don't exactly know." My heart was sad, yet my mind kept retracing to the events of the wash basket lid that happened during the night. I can't explain how I knew it was her, as I didn't see her or sense her, but at that moment of being told she had died, I just knew it was her.

A few months after she died, I began to see shadows walking around my home during the daytime, not just at night. It became a natural occurrence for me, so I just got on with my days. Until one day, a friend came to stay and she saw an elderly woman in my kitchen putting on the kettle. She described my Aunt right down to the walking cane and her limp, and the look she had given her as if to say, "who are you and what do you think you are doing here." I laughed because in my mind's eye I could see the look and her whole mannerisms. Even to this day, some evenings as I sit relaxing I can hear the kettle being turned on as it clicks, but when I go to look, it's not actually on.

Why was it that I was the one who was having these experiences, and why have they not happened before? It all seemed to begin the night my husband died. Was I just creating them, or wishing them into being, or was there a different explanation for all of this? These occurrences were happening before I even knew they had died, so I couldn't have wished it to happen. It was as though something inside of me was sensitive, that it had opened up to a new way of experience. When I look back in hind sight, a veil had been lifted between this reality and the reality of Spirit. It wasn't something that I had chosen, not consciously anyway, yet it was happening in front of me and I wasn't sure how to stop it or even if I could control what was happening.

Memories of my childhood started to flood into my awareness, memories that reminded me of feeling unsafe and scared in my room at night. One memory in particular, when I was about 3 years old, it was in the middle of the night and I was out of bed, standing at the door, looking into the room, crying and yelling out, "leave me alone, go away." It was at this moment that I realized I have always had these recurring moments at night. I Was a very sensitive child, who just knew things about people and situations, even before they did. I found it difficult as a child to sensor what I was feeling about others, and oh boy did it get me into trouble...a lot...

CHAPTER 2

DIMMING THE LIGHT

The light was my own journey and my own unique way of living.

CHAPTER 2

DIMMING OF THE LIGHT

This chapter of my life was a bitter sweet time. I was hit with so many deep emotions through family members dying, yet at the same time, I was experiencing them still being in this reality, even after death. I experienced feelings, energy swirling, shadows and thoughts, as visions of them appeared and disappeared daily.

The following two years after my husband died, my family experienced more deaths. I remember at my Aunts funeral, being very deep in sorrow to the point of noticing that the grief, the tears and the sobbing, was not just for her but also for my husband. The experience of my Aunt dying had triggered all the pain and sorrow that was still within me from my husband's death. Then another death, and another funeral, and another death and another funeral, on and on they went. What was happening? There were six deaths in two years, and before this, none. Every funeral I noticed sadness growing stronger and all the people who had died entered my mind and heart at each funeral. I wondered how anyone could possibly cope with all this grief and sadness. After each funeral, I stepped back into life and was living once again, tucking the grief away in a safe place inside of me.

Around eighteen months after my husband died, I began to notice my breathing would become shallow and tight, especially when I was stressed and busy. This feeling started to happen when I was out, especially in queues at the shop and in the bank. Eventually it would happen when I was in the car, not while the car was in motion, but when I was stationary at traffic lights. I began to surrender to this feeling because I recognized it as panic and anxiety, but I didn't know what to do, or how to stop it. Eventually I gave in and went to my local doctor who prescribed a mild relaxant. I began to take them and within a short while I felt as though I could function normally again.

The trauma had taken a toll on my anxiety, I felt I was becoming reliant on the relaxants, not that I had to take them each day, but I had to know they were with me wherever I went; just in case I needed them, just in case I was out of control emotionally, and just in case I got scared and didn't feel safe. Then I realised, this form of living was not the life I wanted, I didn't want to be reliant on anything or anyone. I went back to my doctor to ask for help. As I walked into the doctor's office I remember thinking, what if he thinks I'm mad? What if he can't help me? I sat down and I said to my doctor, "I can't do this anymore; I want to be normal again." Now, in truth, I really didn't know what that meant as these words flew out of my mouth, and I must say it wasn't spoken in a nice calm manner. It was spoken from a deep strength of a strong conviction and determination.

To my surprise, my doctor understood where I was coming from and all he said was, "would you be willing to see a hypnotherapist?" I heard myself saying, "Anything, anything, I will try whatever it takes to help myself feel calm and normal again." He gave me the referral and within a week I found myself sitting in the waiting room of the Hypnotherapist.

The fear and apprehension I was feeling in the waiting room was so intense that a couple of times I thought I would have to walk out. I held it together, knowing that this was my last chance of sanity. I contained my anxiety until I was ushered into the room. I sat down for a few minutes answering some questions when my tears began to flow. Actually, they fell so fast and strong that I was overwhelmed with how quickly they came out. I was sobbing, yet the doctor had not even asked me anything significant. I was not able to contain my emotions and he just waited, passing me a tissue until I controlled my emotions enough to talk. There was so much emotion bottled up in me that entering this room, with this doctor, gave me permission to release, to let the flood gates open until enough was released that I could be present with the session.

In all I had five sessions with this man, and these five sessions were enough to create within my mind, body, and spirit, a place to go to and calm my mind which then calmed my body sensations, which ultimately calmed my spirit. The most significant session for me was him showing me, and placing within my psyche, a link to take me into a deep meditative state. All I had to do was close my eyes and count backwards from ten to one, breathe deeply, and within moments I would be in a state of relaxation. This state of relaxation was deeper than I had ever been before. As I practiced going to that place within me every day, I began to see a light at the end of the tunnel, and this tunnel was taking me back towards life. The light was my own journey and my own unique way of living.

CHAPTER 3

WINDS OF CHANGE

There is nothing to fear but your own fear, created through your own mind.

CHAPTER 3

WINDS OF CHANGE

I had finally found a place to rest, rejuvenate and recover from what seemed to be a harrowing experience. I had found meditation, and meditation became my Holy Grail of sanity; it allowed a space between my thoughts and fears that was calm and serene. It was through this time in my life that I found devotion, and I devoted some time each day to meditation.

One morning as I entered my daily meditation, I found myself in some kind of vision. Well I thought it was a vision, until I realised that I was actually in the reality of where I was, as though I had been propelled into a different time and space. When I looked around I saw that I was at a funeral, and while everyone was sitting down, I was walking towards the coffin. It was then that I realised I had no control. I tried to stop myself but I couldn't, my body just kept walking. Then I heard within my mind, two people talking to me, "It will be alright, we want to show you something." I felt the presence of two people, one on either side of me walking with me, yet I couldn't see them. It was then that I tried to bring myself out of the meditation and found that I was deeper than I realised. It took a lot of will power before I finally jolted back into the room, on my chair in my lounge room. Needless to say, I stopped meditating from that moment, but my deep insatiable pull for peace of mind eventually pulled me back to meditation.

During my break from meditation, I began to look at my fears and how they control my life. I realised that many times in my life I have stopped myself from growing, changing and venturing out, all because of fear. I decided to go back into the meditation and find out why I was at that funeral, so I sat and breathed and within a short while I was once again at that funeral walking towards the coffin. I was also aware of the two people with me, yet this time I felt comforted and safe with them; even though I never knew who they were, or whether they were spirit or guidance. We walked towards the coffin and as I felt my fear rising within, I also heard the voices say to me, "you have to see what is real." I was afraid to see who would be lying in that coffin, I kept thinking, no, not another person dying, please no. Suddenly I was thrust forward and saw who was in the coffin; it was me lying in that coffin.

I felt relieved, but also confused. Then the voice within spoke to me "there is never anything to fear, as everything is you, and it is always you that you fear, always you that you hide from and always you that you run away from." Suddenly I was out of the meditation, and sitting back in my room. I began to laugh out loud and then cry, I was laughing and crying as I could feel something shifting inside of me. I couldn't help wondering what this experience was for, and as soon as I thought this, the voice within spoke, "there is nothing to fear but your own fear, created through your own mind." It was then that I saw the truth, that when my mind is peaceful I am peaceful, and when my mind is full of thoughts, fears and doubts then my life begins to resemble that.

I never stayed away from meditation again, it actually had the opposite effect on me; I wanted to see more, understand more and experience more through a peaceful mind. Life in general started to change, I felt more open, calm and in control of my life. Finally I was accepting my experiences of spirit contacting me after someone dies. This helped the stages of grief, but truly the ultimate for anyone who is left behind, including myself, would be to have the tangible solid appearance once more.

I still craved this, but deep inside I knew that it was not a possibility in this reality, actually not in any reality, as the body is no longer. The part of them that was solid and of form and touchable, breathable and felt through all sensory perception was no more. This was the sadness that I was still experiencing and I know that if it wasn't for my experiences of spirit being present and the voice within, then I may not have dealt with the grief so easily.

I found meditation easy and calming so I tried not to miss a day. I loved the experience of connection to something greater than me, something that had a bird's eye view of life and the world I was living in. I started to write, to journal what I saw and heard in my meditations, not because I believed it was going to happen, but because I needed to write it down just in case. Eventually I only randomly wrote things down from my meditations, as I began to feel trust in myself, and the voice within.

My journey was mine, and at times I felt alone, not sure if anyone would understand me and my experiences. It was only close friends that I shared with and even then, some of them looked upon me as a bit strange. I was like a fish out of water, trying to find my pond again; where do I fit in? Where's my place in all of this?

My little world became too small for my experiences and I wanted to share them with the world or at least others who were having similar experiences. Through this time of questioning and meditation, I began to notice shops opening up in my neighbourhood which represented the life I was experiencing; full of books of wisdom, crystals for healing, the New Age shops were spreading throughout society. You could find anything from meditation Cds, books, psychic readers, incense and so much more. It was fun, and I felt at home as I wandered through these shops. Finally, I wasn't the only one who was having these experiences.

Then one morning I was feeling a bit melancholy and thinking about my husband in Spirit. I walked into the spare bedroom, opened the wardrobe where his belongings were, picked up his leather jacket from the wardrobe and held it close to me. This was something I would often do when the thought of him not being here pulled me down. His clothes still held his scent on them. These times were comforting and I could feel his presence stronger each time I did this.

After feeling his presence, I felt an urge to go out and visit a New Age shop that had recently opened in the area. I had been there a few times to buy incense, browse and take in the calming feeling of the shop. When I arrived at the shop I was welcomed by a lady who was working that day. I had not seen her in the shop before, but soon found out she was the owner. Being the only customer in the shop we connected and started to chat. She asked me if I wouldn't mind if she practiced some psychometry with me; she is clairvoyant and wanted to expand her gifts for her clients.

Of course, I was happy to oblige and receive a free reading. I gave her my watch and she began to read using psychometry. Only a few moments passed when she looked at me and said, "This man with you, he loves you so much." Here it was again, the same statement from the men at the shop where I worked. She continued saying, "he is telling me about the leather jacket and wants you to know that he watches and knows what you do." Well you could have knocked me over backwards; he really is there, and at every moment. Wow, that was a lot to take in. I felt like an open book and was a bit apprehensive about her continuing. She was answering my deeper queries of wanting to know the truth, yet a part of me wanted to run and hide.

Too late, she continued and what she said next gripped my heart, and my mind propelled me into a spin. She began to speak of my husband's brother who had sadly taken his own life about 6 months earlier. She continued to tell me that his brother had been with him for a while in spirit and was well and happy, but had to move on in spirit to continue his own healing journey. At this moment, she looked at me strangely and asked questions regarding how the brother died and where he was when he died. Then she stopped and told me she knew the brother. Her husband was a good friend of his and they were at the funeral.

I looked at her in disbelief. What a coincidence, and yet deep inside I already knew that even this day was no coincidence. From the leather jacket, to visiting the shop, to us being the only two people in the shop. This was all orchestrated, but not by my conscious mind. She began to share more with me and it was my husband who wanted us to meet and connect. This was when I finally accepted and believed that in Spirit, he was helping me on my journey. I became a frequent visitor to the shop and the owner and I connected deeply, as she also shared with me her own personal loss through death. We united together through our experiences and connected with small groups of like-minded people. This was where the deepening of my spiritual journey began, as confidence and clarity helped me to change my beliefs as I followed the winds of change.

CHAPTER 4
THE 11.11 PHENOMENA

I have learnt over the years that trust is a huge component when working with guidance and the energy fields.

CHAPTER 4

THE 11.11 PHENOMENA

My life was changing. I was finally able to relax, enjoy, and understand myself as a woman, mother and friend. I had realised that for most of my adult life, I was following what others thought I needed to be. I always tried to keep the peace, and calm the environment I was living in, not realising this was for my own sanity and safety. In this period of my life, I was in constant communication with the voice within and my meditations were deep and fulfilling. I finally left a relationship with a man who I stayed with after my husband died. I thought this was my safe place, yet I was never truly happy there. I wanted some form of security for my son after the tragedy of his father dying.

Here I was for the first time in many years, living as a single mum with a teenage child. I felt a connection to life and the unseen; everything that happened came from a deep guidance, as though I had my very own direct link to the universe and God. Creation was simple and easy, where thought would manifest a positive outcome, as my life became my spiritual journey.

Healing through Reiki entered my life in the early years. I began to share with family and friends the gift of Reiki. I set up a healing room in my home which became my sanctuary to meditate in and give Reiki treatments. The energy within my home began to change, as did the guidance through meditation and the voice within. So much was occurring around me and my home, that I felt totally protected and guided. This became so natural for me that I stopped questioning everything and began to trust.

One morning, I woke and walked into my lounge room to see my large clock which sat on the television had stopped; it had stopped at 11.11. This was a battery-operated clock, so I went over to get the old batteries out to change them. I looked at the back of the clock and the batteries were already out and sitting on the television. Instantly I thought it was my son who had taken them out, so I placed them back into the clock, reset the time and checked the batteries were good.

The following day, I walked in from work and was drawn to look at the clock. It had stopped again at exactly 11.11. I went to the clock and the batteries were out and on the television, just like the day before. This time I approached my son and asked him why he kept taking the batteries out of the clock. He looked at me as though I was strange and said, "What are you talking about? I haven't touched the clock." Of course, I didn't believe him as we were the only two people living in the house and it wasn't me. I let it go and got on with my evening and when I woke up in the morning I walked into the lounge room and once again the clock had stopped at 11.11 and the batteries were out. What was happening? My son was still in bed, so now I knew it wasn't him.

The urge to meditate was strong; I sat in my room and dropped into my morning meditation. The meditation started with all the usual feelings, colours and deepening, as I rested internally; stillness surrounded me. An image began to appear in my inner vision. I observed as the vision became clear, it was my grandpa, he was sitting in his wheelchair looking up at me. I heard internally, "it's time for me to go." He didn't speak these words; they came through me, through my own inner voice. I felt in my heart that it was his time to crossover. I spoke to him in the meditation and shared with him "If it is truly your time to go, the family will be alright, and just know you are loved beyond time and space" I felt a calming energy overtake me at that moment and slowly the image of my grandpa began to fade. When the meditation had finished, I contemplated on what I had just seen, heard and spoke and as I do, surrendered this to the universe. I knew the outcome was not in my hands or my grandpa's.

I continued with my day, yet still trying to clear my mind of the experience from my morning meditation. Work was busy and before I knew, it was time for my morning break. Working for family allowed me a bit more freedom than a regular job. I could take my breaks when I wanted as I was the only one in the shop most days. I made my cup of tea, sat behind the counter and enjoyed the moment of having an empty shop.

Without warning, I was engulfed by a smoky white haze, which lingered in front of me for a moment and then disappeared as quickly as it had appeared. I was in a state of shock thinking, what was that? It felt real, like spirit moving in front of me. At that moment the phone rang, I picked it up and it was my dad, he told me that my grandpa had just passed away. Just then, I looked at the clock and it was 11.11am. My mind was all over the place. I was hearing dad's voice telling me this, yet I was taken back to my meditation remembering the message from my grandpa. I put the phone down and had to focus to bring myself back into the workplace, to where I was, and take in the sadness that my grandpa had passed. I wanted to cry, yet felt laughter at the so-called coincidence of timing; so much to contemplate on, and so much to take in. The day continued, I spoke to family members and we all knew it was for the best as Grandpa was old, in a nursing home, and not having a very good quality of life.

It was a long day, but that evening I had already agreed to go to a meditation group with a friend for the first time. I had never meditated with a group before as this was something I did in my own home and within me. We arrived at the group and were greeted by the facilitator, who I had met prior at a psychic fair; he had given me a reading and we connected as though we had known each other before. The evening began, there were twenty of us as we sat in a group to meditate. I enjoyed the guided meditation as this was not something I had a lot of experience doing.

After the meditation, we were asked to share our experiences. I listened as each person shared something. When it was my turn I shared my peace and enjoyment of being guided through the meditation. The facilitator asked if he could share something with me that he had seen through the meditation. He told me that during the meditation, he was asked by his guidance to open his eyes and he saw an elderly man standing behind me. He watched as the spirit of the man kept fading in and out. He felt that this elderly person had not been in spirit very long, as he was having difficulty holding the energy in that density of form. I smiled and shared with him and the group that my grandpa had passed away earlier that day. At that moment, I remembered another "coincidence"; the facilitator's and my grandpa's names were Alex. As I shared this coincidence with the group, we all laughed in awe at the perfectness of the connection, the experiences of the day and the meditation.

After meditation, we all came together for hands on healing. As a Reiki practitioner, I was used to this and was looking forward to my turn. When it was my turn, I lay down and within minutes, was deep and resting inside. I began to feel strange sensations on my face, it felt as though my skin was moving and tingling. At first I just giggled inside, until my friend began to freak out and say, "Oh my God, look at her face, its changing." I didn't know what to think at that moment, I felt fine so I burst out laughing, which bought me back into my body and the group. As I opened my eyes, everyone was staring at me so I asked, "What happened? What did you see?" My friend and Alex, the facilitator, described how my face began to change, predominantly on my jaw and chin. They could see another person's face starting to move in front of mine. I thought this would scare me as I am so used to being in control, yet for some reason it felt right; I was more intrigued than anything. Who was it with me? Was it my grandpa or someone else? Nobody knew, and to this day I still don't know. I have learnt over the years that trust is a huge component when working with energy fields. I realised that while the change was occurring, I was still present, feeling and knowing what was happening, which is most likely why I was so calm.

We stayed back for a chat and coffee. While I was talking to Alex he told me, "during this time in your life, you won't know where the future will take you, but you will experience deep transformations within you that you could not possibly comprehend." I felt a bit overwhelmed and saw a book in my mind that I was reading; it was about a medium and her guide, how she channels him as he comes through her. I reacted rather immaturely at the time and told him, "no way is anybody going to jump into my body and take me over." He looked at me and replied, "I can't say anymore as you're not ready to hear this." He was right, I wasn't ready. I left that night thinking, no way, that is not my journey, even though I loved reading about it and seeing it, but not for me. I never returned to that group.

Even though I never returned to that group, I would often bump into Alex. It seemed that everywhere I went, events, lectures, fairs, he was there. Then I moved interstate. Found like-minded people and connected once more into the new age field, and yet there he was again at every fair I attended. I finally recognised that it wasn't the connection to Alex the man, but my connection to my grandpa Alex that I was not seeing. Once I recognised this within myself, I never saw him again.

One day while I was dusting at home, I picked up my grandpa's photo and heard within, "remember my name, my name is important." My grandpa's name was Alexander Dove Adam. At that moment, I saw a dove in my mind and knew this would be my connection to my grandpa. That evening I held a meditation group. During meditation, my friend was told to open his eyes and he saw a white dove hovering above the group. He shared this with the group and I smiled deeply as I remembered the experience earlier that day with my grandpa. I was venturing deeper, and loved my life, my experiences, and the connections that were always present.

CHAPTER 5

THE RESTING POOL

Resting is a great place to be. It signifies a space in between, where you can rejuvenate, contemplate, and take time away from your life and your mind.

CHAPTER 5

THE RESTING POOL

Resting is a great place to be. It signifies a space in between, where you can rejuvenate, contemplate, and take time away from your life and your mind. We know as human beings that at times we can leave a situation and return to it feeling refreshed and renewed. Other times, leaving a situation does not help and life may feel hopeless. My experience of the resting pool began only a few months after moving interstate, away from my family and my partner's family. Settling in was busy, trying to find work and a permanent residence. Everyday there was something to do or somewhere to go. I began to feel life overwhelming me and distracting me from my inner dialogue and meditation. It was then, that I returned to my morning practice and sat deeply within, to begin each day with peace.

One morning after my meditation, my partner received a phone call from a family member informing us my partner's brother was in hospital after attempting to end his life He was on life support and the diagnosis was not good. The doctors were telling the family that his brain was not responding and was brain dead. This was an emotional time for everyone, especially my partner who could not go see him.

The feeling for me was of being helpless, how could we help? There was nothing we could do except wait. At that moment, my internal guidance showed me to send Reiki energy through an absent healing.

Straight away I sat and tuned into my brother-in-law. Using my training in Reiki 2, I sat and connected with his higher self and began a dialogue that I wrote down. He was communicating with me; I saw him, I felt him and I heard him speak to me. The image in my mind's eye was of a lake, very peaceful and serene, not even a ripple upon it. In the middle of the lake, I saw a small wooden boat and there he was just sitting, looking down. I asked him, "Are you alright?" He told me how he was feeling, what was happening in his life, and that he just wants to rest. After writing this down, I would honour the dialogue and keep the paper work on an altar in my healing room. I continued these over a 24 hour period.

The reports from the hospital were the same; he was brain dead and they were going to turn off life support in the morning. I decided to do one more absent healing before he fully passed over. I sat and went in and again there he was in the boat, resting and as he had told me, needing time out. I continued to write down his thoughts and feelings until I heard "shake, rattle and roll" "shake, rattle and roll" the third time I heard this he looked at me and said, "What do I do? Where do I go?" It was then I realised they were trying to wake him up at the hospital. I was confused as well, what do you say to someone who is transitioning? I said the only thing that came to my mind. "Go to the light" I said. He looked at me and said, "Are you sure?" Well of course I wasn't, but instinctively I repeated it, "Go to the light." Suddenly, the energy connection between us stopped and he was no longer sitting in the boat. Wow, I thought, he's passed over. We waited for the phone call expecting the worse but to our surprise we were told he woke up, opened his eyes and smiled at everyone.

The very next day he walked out of hospital with no adverse side effects. This was a profound moment on my journey, where I now understand that all experiences have an ending that are not consciously known to the mind or body. He didn't know that he would not die; he tried to end his life, yet it was not his time and those that do leave through this process, it's because it was their time.

A few months later he came to visit and I gave him the written dialogue we had in that place on the lake. The usual process was to burn these in a ritual, but for some reason I knew to hold onto them and give him the opportunity to read them. He retired to his room with the Reiki 2 dialogue and when he came out he was struck with such appreciation and shared with me that reading them helped to understand where his life was at that time and how he was feeling. What was written down were the feelings he was having, but wasn't able to express them. I knew in my heart that he was ready to go back to his life and deal with it in a different way.

He changed his patterns, his reactions and how he dealt with life. He did not remember our communication on the lake as it was never in his conscious mind. I understood that where we were in those moments were beyond form and beyond the world we see through the body's eyes. Do I fully understand what happened in the healing process? No, definitely not! Am I meant to understand? No, not at all! All I know, is some human experiences are created and cultivated for reasons that the rational mind may never know. Do we ever really know the outcomes of some experiences? Not really! We look at past experiences and what we have read or heard from others and the world becomes what we take in and believe. It is only when you are right in the middle of a situation that you begin to pray and hope for a positive outcome. It is not always the case that loved ones can return. After my experiences, I can now see that this moment called death is not in our control. We cannot change the moment of death as this is the destiny of the Souls embodiment. Live your life to have a full life, don't focus on trying to keep destiny away, as that is unchangeable.

CHAPTER 6

LOVE APPROVAL & APPRECIATION

I am not really sure what happened that day, but I do know, it had happened within me and I was a different person toward my dad because of it.

CHAPTER 6

LOVE, APPROVAL & APPRECIATION

I had been living interstate, away from my family, for about three years, and could only visit occasionally as it was expensive to fly at the time. I would often connect with my family by phone; my Mum, sisters, and my son who was older now, but the one person I still avoided was my father. Even though I was away from home for a long time, I rarely missed him or needed to talk to him. This was just how it was; I loved him, but didn't feel the need to connect with him.

Then one Christmas day I was sitting outside in the sunshine looking up at the clouds, feeling grateful for my life, my work and my home which was a beautiful healing centre. Suddenly, I felt a shift of energy inside me and heard the inner voice say "it's time for you to go home, back to where you came from." I freaked out. No, why? Why do I have to go? I looked up at the sky and in the clouds; I saw the word freedom appear. It was so clear, as the inner voice said, "It is there you will find your freedom." I just knew I had to go back, I can't explain the feeling and the precise knowing that this was what I had to do.

Here I was living a wonderful life, in my beautiful home where I had created a sanctuary and healing centre, yet I was going back. In no time, I was selling things, making arrangements and before I knew it, I was on the plane. I arrived in winter and it was cold and miserable. Each day I wondered why I was there, what was the freedom that I would encounter, and where was it? I settled in and got on with life, but in the back of my mind I missed my new home, the place that truly felt like home.

Once a week I would visit my mum and hang out with her. Dad was usually out or at golf. I knocked on the door and to my surprise my dad answered. It was awkward, as I said before, I never really connected with him to just hang out and have a coffee. Mum was out shopping, but he opened the door for me to come in. We sat and made idle chit chat, waiting for Mum to come home. He was rather talkative today, sharing his days and what's been happening, when I noticed a shift in him. He seemed to struggle to get certain words out, got agitated and told me, "this happens often now, it must be old age." He continued to tell me how he gets frustrated with Mum, that she is impatient and tries to finish his sentences for him.

I sat listening to my father share this with me;

this probably was the deepest personal conversation I ever had with Dad. He continued to speak to me and share his feelings; it was as though I was a stranger or his therapist, not his daughter. Mum was running late and I had to go, so I thanked Dad for the coffee and chat and left. I left with a different perspective of my dad than the one I arrived with. Something deep had shifted inside of me, my stories of my father and my childhood softened from that day onwards. I am not really sure what happened that day, but I do know, it had happened within me and I was a different person toward my dad because of it.

Each day I meditated and asked for guidance in finding my freedom. All I honestly wanted was to go back to the state I had come from; I loved that place, the tropical warmth and sunshine, the friends I had met and my lifestyle that I left behind. Six months had passed and the decision was made, I was leaving once more to go home to the sunshine. It felt right and I was happy with the decision. I loved my family, yet knew in my heart I didn't have to be right there with them. Was this my freedom? Who knows? It just felt right.

Arriving back, I had to stay with friends until I decided where I wanted to live. I didn't have to be in any one place or close to anyone in particular. This felt like the freedom I was shown. Free to come and go and travel to wherever I wanted, but the greatest freedom at that time was the healing that had taken place within me, regarding my relationship with my father.

Resting in my room I felt the pull to go within, to meditate. I surrendered my situation to guidance and asked to be shown where I was meant to be and live. I heard the telephone ring in the house and my friend answered it. I heard her talking and laughing to whoever was on the phone, and I smiled to myself as I sat deep in meditation yet was aware of life around me. After the meditation, I ventured out of my room and my friend asked me if I knew yet where I wanted to live. I said, "No, funny you should ask that, I just surrendered this question to my guidance." She laughed and asked, "Would you like to move up North as my friend lives in a share home and asked if I knew of anyone who was looking for a room." I wasn't sure if this was where I needed to go, but the synchronistic connection was too good not to take a look.

The very next day I drove north, looked at the room and the stunning property it was on and instinctively felt that this was my next home. Before I had time to think about it, I was moving once more and found myself in the mountains on a glorious property with like-minded people. Life was simple, free and easy. Nature became my home as I was surrounded by creatures great and small, grew vegetables, and lived in an eco-home with vegetarians. What more could a spiritual girl ask for.

Spending time in nature had given me a deep connection to the peace that resides within me, not the peace that I was searching for in the outside world. I was consciously aware of animals and birds that lived on the property and would feel their presence even before I saw them. Meditation was deep in this beautiful place, as I worked, lived and contemplated life from a different perspective.

Since moving to the mountain I found myself reflecting on my time spent with family, especially my mum and dad. One evening as I was sitting on the balcony enjoying the cool night air after a hot summer's day, I saw a large white owl fly directly in front of me before disappearing. How beautiful I thought as I went inside to bed. The next evening while sitting outside, the white owl appeared again, flying low right past me. The following evening, I had hoped the owl would return and it did, but this time it landed on the ground in front of me and began to sing. I looked at the owl in awe at the beauty and size of this magnificent creature. I shrugged my shoulders and spoke to the owl telling it that I didn't know what it was trying to tell me. It then flew away. This was my last encounter with the white owl on this property.

The very next day I received a phone call that my dad had been taken to hospital in a serious condition and may not survive. I was in shock, my dad had never been sick a day in his life, how could this be happening. It was then I remembered an experience with another white owl and being told that in Native American lore a white owl can represent physical death coming. Of course, the owl was so persistent and was trying to show me something but I was not aware at that moment to connect it to death, especially not my dad's.

Dad passed and I was back in my home town once more to say goodbye. It all happened so fast that before I knew it I was home in my bedroom trying to make sense of what had happened. I felt lost and scared, and didn't understand how from one day to the next, change could be so dramatic. This brought up my anxiety as I had no say in this, no control. I couldn't even say goodbye, it happened so fast. I was still grieving, yet had to go to work, live normally and continue as though nothing had happened.

Whenever my anxiety is triggered, I know it is time to delve deeper into meditation, to clear my mind and calm the effects the mind has on my body. It was then that I was shown the moment of listening and being told to go back to my home town the year before. I cried and was so grateful to be able to spend time with Dad before he passed. If it wasn't for guidance that Christmas day, I may not have seen him before he passed and would not have the deeper understanding of who he was as my father.

My heart had finally healed some of the grievances I kept hidden away regarding Dad, always judging him for his lack of emotional support and connection. Then after the time spent with him before he died, I saw Dad in a different light. This never stopped the process of grief, and I will tell you that no matter how spiritual you are or how wise you have become, the grieving process will still happen but you begin to heal quicker and easier through the process. Once I recognised the orchestrated moments that led to me connecting back to Dad, I noticed that I was much more caring in my heart and mind for my father and the life we shared together.

I appreciated memories and the little things he would do for me and everyone, and I saw that in his own way, he did approve of some of my decisions that I had made in my life, maybe not all of them, but some of them. Finally, I knew deep in my heart that he loved me as his daughter and through me I am finally honouring my father by being a success in my life and my business.

CHAPTER 7

FADING MEMORIES

The Soul never dies, it is energy, and it is real, yet not solid or form.

CHAPTER 7

FADING MEMORIES

When someone we love dies, it is important for those left behind to hold onto a memory, an image or even to hear their voice for one last time. This helps to keep them close, to know that they are still reachable, and not forgotten. We know that time can be the healer with these difficult emotions, yet time can also fade the connection that we had to the person we knew and loved dearly. We assemble altars to honour our loved ones, to connect easily on a visual sense, but the form, the touch, the physical, this is the hardest to let go of, yet it is the first piece that is disconnected from the person you loved. Once this is gone, the rational mind does not understand or know how to connect to the elements of energy. Before you know it, time has begun the rubbing out process of the solid form that was so tangible and visible. As hard as this seems, this is the letting go process, the process of healing.

Imagine if you were to understand that the body is not who you are and the Soul was the energy that embodied it. Therefore, it is the Soul that you are looking for, the Soul that you miss and the Soul that you love. It was the Soul's energy that transferred into the body and lived through the body. The Soul never dies, it is energy, it is real, yet not solid or form.

Let me share my experience of seeing Soul just when I thought memory was fading. It had been a few years since my husband had passed and I could finally reminisce with friends and family in a positive way. I was living with a friend in-between relationships and enjoying a relaxed life with spiritually like-minded people. One evening I felt a bit lonely and retired to my bedroom early. I sat on my bed and just looked around the room, not really thinking about anything or anyone. I thought about my past and the people who journeyed with me and the ones who had left. I reached into my wardrobe and took out a box filled with over twenty years of photos. I began looking through them and laughed at the old photos, yet also felt sadness and surprise. Then I realised my deceased husband was nowhere to be seen amongst all those photos.

I remembered sorting through my photos after he died and making an album up for our son. I didn't want them as I was still angry at him. Angry at our volatile marriage and the deep emotions that were so raw and still hurting, that I gave his photos away. Now I wanted to see him, to feel him, to hear him once more. Finally, I found a photo with him in the background. I felt I needed to have a deeper connection with him as I realised in that moment, I missed him. I missed him in every part of my life and my Soul. As I looked at the photo I spoke to him out loud, "where are you? I can't see you, I can't hear your voice anymore and I miss you." I put the photos away and fell asleep.

I woke the next morning without a thought of the night before and my emotional outburst; I was used to having these moments. It was a rainy day and as I drove to work nothing appeared different, just the usual traffic jams as I patiently sat in the traffic. The rain had kept the morning rush of customers away, which was always a great time to clean, dust and rearrange furniture on the shop floor.

I looked up as the doorbell rang indicating someone had entered the shop. I went to the counter to see a man standing there looking a bit frazzled. He asked for directions as he was lost and needed to get to a job interview. The first thing I noticed about this man was a black t-shirt he was wearing that said Humpty-Doo Pub. I giggled to myself as I read the t-shirt, remembering my husband had mentioned visiting this place just before he travelled to see me and my son.

As I talked to the man trying to help him with directions, I noticed a familiar memory; he reminded me of my husband. He was dressed in jeans, a black t-shirt, wearing black sunglasses, and looking a bit rough around the edges. He had long shoulder length hair, a goatee beard, and tattoos on his arms. This encounter was beginning to feel odd because I had just described my husband. He took his sunglasses off and it looked as though he had been in a fight. I asked him what happened. He shared that he was new to the city and was jumped last night by a couple of men, was beaten and had his wallet stolen. I gave him the directions he needed and he left the shop. It wasn't until he left that I was shown the whole picture.

My husband also had long hair, a goatee beard, wore a lot of black, dark sunglasses, and had tattoos on his arms. He had stayed at Humpty Doo, was also mugged and had his wallet stolen, and received a broken nose and black eye from a similar experience in the same place and town. I was shocked at how similar they were and wondered if this was some sort of message or synchronistic event. However, as the day progressed, this experience began to slip out of my conscious mind and the duties of work took over.

Later that afternoon the coffee man came in as he had finished his rounds for the day. He just wanted to talk and share his feelings about his pet ferret that was dying. We spoke in depth about his ferret and how upset he was to let it go. We talked about the letting go process and how he was struggling with the final decision to have it put down.

Our discussion changed as he talked about his belief in life after death. He shared with me his experience with his grandfather who had passed over and how he feels him and knows that he is still with him. The decision to end his pets suffering was partly because his grandfather's spirit helped him to see that the body can and will suffer but the spirit becomes pure energy and does not suffer anymore.

I sat and listened to his version and his beliefs around death, acknowledging the connection to my own beliefs of death and life after death. He left the shop, and I sat and thought about my husband and the coincidences that related to my own personal experiences. I shook my head and began to close the shop for the day and start the long drive home in heavy traffic.

When I arrived home, my house mate who is a Psychic reader was still working with a client. I gave them space to finish and went to my room. At this stage I wasn't thinking about my day's discussions and synchronistic events. The long drive home had taken care of any thoughts other than traffic and being alert. My housemate finished her reading and called me into the kitchen to join them for a coffee and chat.

The conversation was light hearted, funny and easy. Then it began to change as my friend's client shared with us her feelings regarding her step father whose name was the same as my deceased husband; and how his brother had recently committed suicide. I listened as her guilt came out. She wanted to help him, because she lived close by and felt maybe she could have helped somehow.

I began to feel uncomfortable. Everything she shared was an exact experience in my life with my husband and his brother. My husband's name, his brother had taken his life. Back then, I too felt guilty, that maybe I could have helped as I was nearby the day it happened.

I had to leave the room. My body was shaking and vibrating, this was too close to home. I excused myself and went to my room, sat on my bed and called out to the universe, to my husband in Spirit, "What is going on?"

A voice spoke to me very clearly and instantly knew it was my husband. He said to me, "you ask me where I am, I can't see you anymore, I can't hear you anymore. I am still here, I have never left. I am in everyone you see, and in every element of your experiences. Just ask and I will be there, weaving within the frame of form and experience. I am not the body so you cannot see me as a body, but that does not mean I have left. No matter where you are, I am there."

I cried, I laughed, and I was so humbled and excited by the day's experiences now that I understood them. I fell asleep feeling connected, and supported, knowing that the truth of all my beliefs about death were beginning to appear in my life. Life is a continuum from one reality into another, yet all realities are here in this one moment, this one space.

CHAPTER 8

LUCY

*This experience for me was divine,
humbling and something I have
cherished in my heart all these years.*

CHAPTER 8

LUCY

Imagine if you had to live with different degrees of illness throughout life. How would you cope, if you began the journey with cancer as a child?

I met Lucy while she was going through treatment for a brain tumour at the age of forty-one. Her journey with cancer began at the age of six when she was diagnosed with bone cancer in her knee. The doctors removed her entire leg as a precaution. For many years, she would have regular checks and at the age of thirty-two, Lucy found a lump in her breast. Once more, Lucy had surgery and radiation. Eight years later, a lump appeared on the back of her upper arm; more surgery and more radiation. One year later, Lucy's brain functions began to deteriorate. Her memory was affected and she found it difficult to find the right words during conversation. Lucy underwent another procedure to remove the tumour in her brain. This never stopped Lucy as she attended university, obtained a science degree, and worked as a Microbiologist. Later in her adult life, she furthered her studies to produce a second degree in IT. Lucy was the most humble, caring, and fearless woman I have ever had the privilege of knowing.

Lucy's family were very supportive throughout her life. They were from a modest Italian family with a strong religious background. Lucy was the youngest of three siblings and her closest ally was her oldest sister who doted on her. Lucy's brother was also steadfast in his strength of will to help his sister, no matter when or how this looked. In fact, the whole family had taken up the crusade of helping Lucy through her life with cancer.

I met Lucy through her sister-in-law who was attending my weekly meditation group. She asked if I could help Lucy to understand the spiritual aspect of healing, as she was beginning to look for alternative help. My first meeting with Lucy and her siblings was beautiful. I sat and listened to Lucy talk about her journey with the medical system and how lately, she was disappointed in the answers and guidance she was getting from main stream medicine.

We talked about the mind and beliefs, as I shared with her, "when we judge something, it persists in our life and we are never accepting of others and ourselves." This was the moment I saw the truth in Lucy's eyes, the truth that deep down she had already found an understanding of her illness. It was at this moment I shared with her, "I am not here to heal you, as that is not my job. I am here to help you." I told Lucy that my presence here is to help her come to terms with herself, her suffering, and to clear any beliefs or judgements that she may have, about herself and her life.

The first few sessions were focused around talking to each other, and how they were coping, not just Lucy but her family as well. Lucy made this very clear from the beginning that she wanted everyone to feel good about the sessions. For me, it was important to create a calming experience for everyone. This family had never sat with meditation before, except for the sister-in-law and occasionally Lucy. Asking them to lie down on the floor with pillows and cushions was very foreign for some of them. I explained that we would enter a Yoga Nidra meditation, where they would find a word within their mind that for them meant healing, relaxation, letting go, or whatever they desired to have as an outcome. This word would become what we call a resolution for the individual, and throughout the meditation we would bring this word into the awareness for healing.

I sat and watched each family member drop deep into their body. The experience for me was divine, humbling and something I have cherished in my heart all these years. We would giggle as they each shared their experience; including the brother who always thought he fell asleep during the meditations until one night he realised he was actually not asleep but relaxed.

The stages of Lucy's cancer were quickening, and it wasn't long after these evenings that she could no longer walk and come to the house for our nights together. I had been using Reiki healing in my own life and with clients for over twelve years when I met Lucy, and asked if I could have a photo of her to continue the connection and healing process through absent healing. While the physical connection was not possible, I was still able to connect and hear Lucy's voice talking to me. In between the absent healings, I placed her photo on my meditation altar at home.

My training in absent Reiki healing was about connecting to the higher self of the individual and having a conversation with them. Through this, I was able to write everything down and give to Lucy at every gathering.

The next stage of Lucy's journey took place in hospital. She told her family that it was imperative the healing sessions would continue. Each week I would be picked up by her Sister-in-law and driven to the hospital. We all sat, and dropped deeply together as we all placed our hands on Lucy for support and healing. Lucy was always smiling after the healing, and I sat and watched the family connect with their sister not just as a physical presence but as a deeper energy presence.

Eventually, Lucy went home so the family could

look after her in her own environment. The family home was near the city and once again I would be picked up and taken to see Lucy. When we arrived at the house, the aromas of cooking would waft into Lucy's room as her Mamma helped in the only way she knew how, through food. After the session, we would all sit in the kitchen area and laugh, eat and be merry. Lucy's Mamma was happy because her children and grandchildren were happy by being with each other after the healings. I never once saw the family disagree where Lucy wanted to go with our sessions.

One evening as we left the house, I could see in my mind's eye an elderly lady bending over the herb garden. She was not present in life, but she was in Spirit. I heard the name Lucia, "I am Lucia and she is named after me." She continued picking herbs from the garden and told me that she is with Lucy helping her from Spirit. I told the family what had happened and they confirmed this was Lucy's grandmother, whom Lucy was named after and she loved being in the garden.

Each week we came together to share, Lucy was quiet yet still smiling. She could no longer speak to communicate. I would bring into the room the absent healing I had written that week. Lucy wanted me to read it out loud to the family, and I realised that most of what was written down were the unspoken words she needed the family to hear. There were times when Lucy would laugh, and times she would cry as she nodded her head in agreement with the written words.

The theme for a majority of the absent healings was around acceptance. That Lucy had accepted and recognised the journey she had to take in this life. Most of all, she wanted her family to know this and for them to also be ok with where she was and what was happening inside of her.

One evening as we all sat and placed hands upon Lucy, energy moved through the room and into each one of us. This energy was calming and surreal as it appeared to engulf the room. When we opened our eyes, we looked upon each other and smiled, as though we knew something magnificent had just entered the room. On the way home that evening my friend asked me what it meant. I shared with her that the family had finally come to an acceptance of Lucy's life within each of them. Now it was out of our hands, she will either come back from this or she will leave the body.

A few days later, I was sitting at my computer and felt energy behind me. I quickly swung around and no one was there. I continued writing and felt the energy again. This time as I turned around, I looked at my altar which sits behind me and looked at the photo of Lucy. I stared at the photo with disbelief, as the image of Lucy slowly disappeared before my eyes. Lucy was fading from the photo and I felt a deep knowing within me, that she had passed. Lucy had finally left the body and was sharing this with me. Not long after, her sister-in-law called and informed me that Lucy had died peacefully that day.

The experience of being with Lucy and her family helped me to see that acceptance is a big component in the passing over process. Not just the acceptance of the individual passing, but it is the acceptance from family and friends that ultimately helps the process. Some of us experience letting go as an uncomfortable idea, and cling onto old familiar memories not wanting life to finish, either their own or another's. It is natural to grieve and not let go; do not even try to deny this process within you. Eventually you will come to an acceptance of the dying process, especially if you have deep moments to share and come together with the person dying.

Acceptance can be met in any moment before the end, if you have time, space, and an open heart; you can often help the person dying to come to terms with it also. Not everyone will be fortunate enough as Lucy's family were to be with their loved ones as they themselves heal and accept the outcome. Sometimes it can be sudden and there is a different healing approach needed. Other times it can be weeks and the family and patient are still trying to come to terms with the sudden onset of illness that can take a life in such a short time. No matter what your experience is, the outcome will be acceptance. Always remember that there are no time limits for the grieving process, and the many stages of grief can last for weeks, months or even years.

Allow yourself the depth of healing needed and remember to notice how you are accepting the finale, or how much longer you will need, before acceptance enters. For some there may never be a complete acceptance, especially with a sudden death. Just know that you are going through a deep transition, a deep letting go. Not a letting go of memories, or experiences, but a deep letting go of the body and the tangible touch that you relied upon. Your acceptance isn't on the death itself but the change of form and how you can interact with them now.

CHAPTER 9

TRUTH REVEALS ITSELF

*Every Soul has embodied with a gift.
The gift is not about changing the
world outside of you, it is changing
the frequency within you.*

CHAPTER 9

TRUTH REVEALS ITSELF

Throughout my journey there have been numerous insights that deepened my awareness through the understanding of life and death. Over the next few years, my life witnessed a reprieve from surges of intense heartfelt experiences. The void from external experiences allowed a sense of calm, peace and compassion to define itself as an internal feeling which is not based upon external stimuli.

I sat with this feeling as I entered work on a Monday morning. Relaxed and sitting with my never ending list of things to do, my phone rang and I was surprised to hear my sister's voice. I heard her say, "Mum has had a stroke", yet I was not prepared for what I heard and it took a few seconds to register in my mind, my heart and my soul. I was confused and my heart began to race as I asked her to repeat what she had said. She repeated the words, "Mum has had a stroke." This was something I never thought my mum would experience. I hung up the phone and felt the wave of fear and emotion rise within me. I waited for the next call when my sister arrived at the hospital. My phone rang and my worst fear had been confirmed. The doctor had asked that family be called in as it was not looking good.

My priority was to get to my mum as quickly as possible my dilemma was that I lived in another state, over a thousand miles away from my hometown. I got to my house and broke down as I lay in my husband's arms. Then my instinct, and overdrive mode, as I call it, kicked in. I had to get a flight home that day and it was already lunchtime. Guidance was with me this day as I found a flight within a few hours. Relief was felt as the flight was booked and I knew I would be there that evening.

While waiting for my flight, I could feel my body shaking on the inside. My mind was giving me fearful thoughts, yet I noticed a wave of calmness wash over me in between the shaking. I knew that Mum's condition was serious, that she was not very stable, yet my guidance kept repeating, "Time will tell." There were moments in the airport lounge when I was aware of my energy field intermingling with my mum's. My head would become heavy with thickness of pressure. I went to the bathroom and released it as I cried.

Waiting patiently for my flight which seemed to be a lifetime away, I was aware of guidance moving into my energy field. I saw images and recent memories moving across my mind. The first image

I was shown was from a dream from the Friday evening before. In the dream, I was in Mums garden looking at the plants and trees. The feeling was that of reminiscing. I walked inside the house and found myself needing to walk into each room and take another look. I sensed there were other people in the house yet I could not see anyone. I walked into the lounge room and there was Dad sitting on a chair. I thought this was odd as Dad had passed away many years before. I remembered something else was happening, the feeling of packing up the house. I looked at Dad and asked, "Why are we packing up the house Mums not dead?" He didn't speak he just looked at me and then the dream ended. Dreams can be so profound, yet most of my dreams are not remembered once I wake. Only the ones I need to remember stay with me, and sometimes guidance randomly triggers them for me to learn more about a deeper experience I am having.

I always carry a writing journal when I fly, therefore managed to document what I was shown. More memories began to form in my mind's eye. I saw my body's experiences over the last ten days. These had been extreme to the point that I had to stop and really look at why my body was having these experiences. I saw that my entire left side of the body was simultaneously blocking, aching and feeling tight. It began in my left tear duct and went into the left side of the head, face, neck, and continued to my toes, feeling like aches and sciatica.

I am very mindful that each event that brings change to my life usually begins with this process as my body throws itself out. These bodily changes were not there to prevent what was coming; they were beginning the process inside me to adjust to the forthcoming changes. I am not God and I cannot change the time of someone's death or my own; that is destiny, the moment the Soul has chosen to depart.

The next memory that passed through my awareness was the day before Mum had the stroke. I met a friend for coffee, and was chatting when she asked me the most bizarre question, "Do you have Bell's palsy Caroline?" I laughed at her, yet felt confused at the same time.

I asked her why she thought that and she shared with me, "sitting here in this close proximity, the left side of your face looks slightly drooping." I was laughing now and I just put it down to the effects of my left side feeling weakened by the shifts that were happening.

I began to feel emotional and agitated as I drove home after my conversation at the coffee shop. By Sunday, my body began to feel release, but was not quite healed. My husband laughed at me as I lay on the bed trying to get comfortable. I was lying on my back with my hands on my heart. He said, "You look as though you're dead lying in that position." We both laughed and fell asleep.

That night was the Sunday when Mum had her

stroke and I was oblivious to what had happened. The entire night I was agitated and felt anxious, waking up randomly through the night, startled and fearful. It wasn't until I arrived at the hospital that I was told she had the stroke around 6pm on Sunday evening, and was not found until Monday morning.

I continued to write in my journal until I boarded the plane. Once on the plane, I dropped into myself to bring about a sense of order and peace under these very stressful circumstances. Connecting internally, I heard guidance clearly as the voice spoke to me, "these experiences are a natural part, the evolution of a Souls journey." The voice continued explaining, "Energy has no container, and is not held into form like the body and the world you see. Therefore, there is no separation between your energy field and your mothers. Every Soul has embodied with a gift and this is your Soul's gift. The gift is not about changing the world outside of you, it is changing the frequency within you." My flight was over; I had finally arrived in my home town where I was born.

Walking into the hospital was surreal as this was the same hospital that I was born in. While looking for the room, I had a déjà vu moment as I walked into the same ward I gave birth to my son in. I entered her room and saw family members with Mum; she was lying on the bed as if sleeping. After the relatives left, the doctor informed me and my sisters that Mum had a major bleed in the brain and unfortunately there was no coming back from the severity of it.

My three sisters and I sat with Mum, watching her breathing without a machine and questioning the doctor's diagnosis. She looked peaceful and would move and moan when touched. This gave us a window of hope to hold onto, something we all needed to stop from breaking down.

As I sat watching Mum, I felt guidance move into my energy field. A memory from a few years earlier filled my mind. I saw myself receiving a reading from a clairvoyant. I remembered what she told me years earlier, that I would be going back to my home town, to help an elderly lady transition to the other side. She also told me that I must remember to come back. I knew then, it would be my mum because I would not have the pull to do this for anyone else in my home town.

Now here I am, many years later looking at my mum and knowing this was the moment the clairvoyant saw. The dots connected, and I realised the truth, Mum had already begun her process and she was not coming back to us.

CHAPTER 10

TAKING MY MOTHER HOME

Energy shifted and as I looked at Mum I could see the realisation on her face that she was not coming back.

CHAPTER 10

TAKING MY MOTHER HOME

Each and every one of us has different belief systems, and ways of dealing with our own personal emotional states and experiences. My way was to look at the situation through energy healing. My life since my husband's death has led me on a path of personal healing. This way of living for me was very satisfying as I began to understand who I am through the field of vibration, energy, meditation and Reiki healing. My family and sisters were aware of my life and how different my approaches to emotions were to their own. I tried not to force my beliefs upon them, but sometimes my excitement appeared to be pushy and authoritative.

I felt the pull to drop in and place my hands on Mum for healing. I shared this with my sisters and began a journey that unravelled many truths and disbeliefs regarding the Spirit's journey home. I placed my hands on Mum and connected. Before I had time to drop in, I was in a vision and saw Mum outside in her garden.

Mum loved her garden it was her very own sanctuary, so it was not a surprise to see her there. As I looked closer she was crouched down and appeared frightened. I tried to coax her out when she said to me, "I'm scared, I'm nervous, I don't know what to do, I don't know where to go." I sensed that Mum knew something was wrong and that she wasn't herself. She reminded me of a frightened child hiding from something or someone. I kept reassuring her that everything will be alright and she asked, "How can you be sure?" Finally, after much persuasion she stood up and talked to me about her garden. Telling me that she had not finished in her garden today, she just couldn't get to all of it. We walked around her garden talking about her plants just as we do when I visit Mum.

The energy in the vision changed. Mum looked at me and said, "I don't like not knowing, not knowing scares me." I knew she was now talking about the hospital and what was happening to her body. She continued to express her feelings, "Damn this body of mine, so very frustrating." In the same breath, she asked, "Why are you here again? Why did you come?" I shared with her I was here to help and she replied, "Why, what do I need to understand?" I observed that Mum was now shifting between noticing she was not really at home, then acting as though this place was her reality. I briefly shared with Mum that soon there will be some choices for her to make. "Choices, what choices?" she asked. I knew in my heart Mum was not ready to take in the fullness of her experience, so we went inside the house and sat down for a coffee.

Inside the vision, I felt another shift in energy and saw Dad standing by their bedroom door. I said to Mum, "Look, Dads here." She looked puzzled and asked, "Where? Where is he?" I looked back towards my dad and he began to talk to me; not in an external voice but inside my mind. I heard him say, "Your mother's not ready, she can't see me yet."

Then I heard Mums voice inside my head, "Total annihilation, there is no way of coming back." She continued and told me she felt trapped, "But I have always felt trapped, story of my life." Mum appeared agitated and scared once more, and then guidance shared with me, "Your mother is beginning to understand what has happened to her." Mum realised that she needed to go beyond her home, she looked to me and said, "No I don't do I? I'm scared, don't tell me I have to go beyond what I know and love." I told Mum that we were all with her. As she began to cry I reassured her that she would not be alone. She calmed herself and asked to be left alone now. I could see that time was needed for her to process everything that was happening. I disconnected energetically from Mum and had time to process my own emotions throughout the night.

Arriving at the hospital early, I connected in with Mum and within moments I could hear Mum talking but could not see her. After a minute or two

I was seeing and hearing Mum. She told me she had been resting, "I don't really like the way you are all fussing over me, it doesn't feel right having you do that to me." I shared with Mum our fussing over her was our way of dealing with what had happened.

Mum seemed a lot stronger internally than the day before. I could feel that she was beginning to process where she was and what was happening to her. Then without any warning, Mum was standing close to me right at my side. It surprised me as I did not see any movement from my eyes perspective. I felt another energy shift and realised we were no longer in Mum's house. Essentially, we weren't anywhere; there were no objects, no sky, or no ground beneath our feet. We appeared to be in a place of no beginning and no end. The communication with Mum became more telepathic now, I could hear her voice within my mind, and she heard my thoughts without me having to speak them. Mum asked, "How long do you think it will be?", as we seemed to be waiting for something. I felt in my heart she wanted to know how long before she dies. Of course, I didn't know the answer and shared that with her.

I felt a lot of pressure in my head and had to ask energetically for this to be lifted. Mum communicated that she was not feeling uncomfortable anymore. She began to ask what we were waiting for but then started to laugh as she saw the irony in her question.

Energy shifted and I felt guidance enter as they

told me, "Your mother will soon begin a deeper journey." They showed me a memory from the movie Field of Dreams where the main character built a baseball field in the middle of his corn field and waited for the Spirits of past baseball players to appear. I knew there was a considerable amount of energy with us now in this void, but Mum needed more time before she could accept what was happening; with her acceptance she would be able to see Dad and the others. I shared this with Mum but she was worried she might not be able to see them. Suddenly two chairs appeared and we were sitting down without actually sitting down. Everything just occurred and happened through me, not by me.

Mum still could not see anything accept the open space, the void. She became agitated so I helped her to relax and believe in herself. Another shift in energy and my grandmother, my mum's mother, appeared in front of us. She spoke with me and stated, "This is part of your soul's destiny and you are the one who has to bring her home." It was at this moment that I broke down, I cried and my sister who was in the room with me tried to bring me back asking if I was alright. I gestured to her that I was ok and not to worry. I asked my grandmother, "How am I supposed to do that?" She looked deep into my eyes smiling and I felt her within me as I heard, "You are already bringing her home." As I looked away from my grandmother, I saw my mum also looking; she could now see her mother. Then her entire family appeared, all of them including ancestors that she would not recognise. My mum was now seeing her entire family for the first time in over sixty-five years. My mum's family were killed during World War 2 and only her and her father survived. Mum could see them, yet she was not moving toward them, not even to her own mother. I heard Mum say, "There is so much to share but where to start I don't know. I just want it to stop, it's too much. It's too much for one person."

When I was younger, Mum would sometimes try to share her pain and suffering of the war but would always end with, "You don't know, you will never know. It was too much for one person to go through alone." Mum was beginning to feel uncomfortable with them all there and began to get angry with them. The energy shifted and I heard a voice say, "We need to move on now." I could not see anyone but we began to move as though we were on a conveyer belt. Mum was feeling uncomfortable as she did not know what else would happen or who else would appear. She looked at me and asked, "Do I have to see anymore? I don't want to see anymore." I calmed Mum by putting my arm around her so she could feel safe.

As we moved along, random images appeared old things and moments from Mum's life. The imagery was stationary and it was us that were passing them by, yet there was nothing moving us along. It reminded me of the many movies I had watched about judgement day where you get to look back on your life before entering heaven. Mum had calmed once more and became excited saying, "This is good, what's next?" No sooner had Mum spoken these words, I heard the name of my dad's mother's family name. I saw my nana before us and other family members from Dad's side appeared. Mum became emotional as this was the only family she really knew and spent many years with them before they passed. Her emotions shut the images down, she turned it off somehow. "Tiny bits" she said, "Tiny bits at a time now." I again felt pressure in my head when Mum looked at me and said, "You just don't know what this feels like."

As Mum was feeling uncomfortable and I was trying to cope with everything from my perspective, we just sat in silence for a while. Then, an enormous white light appeared in front of us. It startled me and Mum with its size and especially how bright it was. At first, I could not look at the light, it was so bright I had to squint my eyes because they were hurting. Mum looked at me and asked, "Is that real?" She was staring at the light now and I told her it was definitely real. Guidance came once more and explained to me that the light was consciousness. It also appeared to have no beginning and no end, just like the space we were in. Mum asked, "Will it stay?", "Yeah, I think it will", I replied. Mum seemed alright with the light being there and wanted to continue to see what was next. Not me though, I needed to end this connection and take time out to process, so I disconnected at this point.

Later that afternoon I connected back to Mum. As I closed my eyes and placed my hands on Mum, I was instantly returned to the same place where I had left her. As we sat together she said to me, "Remember we're taking tiny steps now." I felt a presence close to me but was not able to see anything or anyone. I felt a bit distracted from Mum when I heard a voice within say, "Das ist gut" which is German for its good. Then I heard, "Only God knows the outcome now." Mum looked at me and said, "So no more tears, don't you think I have cried enough in this lifetime. Tiny steps, remember tiny steps." I began to feel pressure in my head again. I noticed that every time Mum was distressed I felt her pain. Mum continued to chat with me saying, "Don't worry it won't last. Decisions, I know I have to make decisions now." Mum seemed curious and was asking a lot of questions and asked if anyone really knew what the outcome would be. Mum said to me, "Sincere, sincere. It's nice that you are all trying to help me."

We were still in front of the light and the relatives were there watching but not coming forward. Mum wanted to know if it was time yet, I didn't know what she meant so I didn't answer her. Another shift in energy and more of Dads relatives appeared. Mum still did not want to go to them. As they appeared,

Mum turned to me and said, "Tough times ahead, it doesn't have to be tough. My whole life, all I wanted was to be happy and nothing else mattered. It's been hard for me, I don't know if anyone really understood that I was happy and content in my home and my garden." Every time Mum spoke now, I could feel what she meant through the words. I felt her happiness living the way she had been living.

She asked, "Do you really believe there is more than what we are seeing here?" I answered "Definitely. There is so much more than this, and soon we will see." Mum voiced her concern, "it is hard being here because what you are seeing in the hospital is worse than what I am experiencing here."

The energy around us began to shift once more. It was different this time, the light felt brighter, more mesmerising. I looked over at Mum and she was also staring at the light, her face glowing as she looked in awe of the light. I could see the rays of light touching her face and she was soaking them into her. The voice said to me, "She is attaching to the rays." The feeling was that Mum was finally finding herself in the presence of the light and the relatives.

What surrounded us now was warmth and glowing feelings that emanated from the inside out. It was then I heard, "Your Mother now understands." Mum looked at me at that moment and said, "I'm beginning to understand now." I nodded to Mum because I too understood the significance of this moment. For me the recognition of the light not being separate from us was deep. Mum was glowing now and said, "There is nothing more brilliant."

An image appeared in my mind. It was a Maypole with different strands of material hanging from the top of the pole. These strands were different energies that connected to each and every one of us. They absorbed everything, including our emotions. I saw that the light was absorbing Mums energy and emotions as they entered the atmosphere. Then I heard, "Total annihilation, total annihilation." I looked at Mum and felt a pull to end the session for the time being. I left Mum sitting in that place with the light embracing her.

I was still next to Mum with my eyes closed and my hands on her, when my sister said, "Oh my God did you see that?" I quickly opened my eyes and looked at her. "What?" I asked, "What did you see?" Sister number three said, "Something just came out of the top of her head, it looked like a hazy white thing, like energy waves about two feet high. What happened?" I knew deep in my heart that she witnessed our mother's Soul leaving the body. When I told her, she was in disbelief, "But she is still here and still breathing." I shared with her that the Soul can leave before the body breaks down completely and stops breathing. The body can still function, it didn't mean that Mum was not present but she was getting ready to leave.

Arriving at the hospital the following morning I

was faced with the deeper truth that Mum was not coming back from her stroke. The nurse shared that her vitals were weakening and her response to touch and stimuli were lessening. In my heart, I knew she was leaving her body but it was still a difficult moment to adjust to.

After the early morning frenzy in the room with family members and coffee breaks, once again I was sitting with sister number three and Mum. We were sitting peacefully with Mum when we both experienced an energy enter the room. I felt I needed to go into meditation as the energy was drawing me within. I sat next to Mum and placed my hand on her shoulder. I looked over at my sister and she was curling up on the chair and closing her eyes. The room was very peaceful and calming. We both stayed like this for about thirty minutes. When I felt the pull to open my eyes, I looked at my sister and she was also opening her eyes. We looked at each other and together spoke how peaceful the feeling was.

It was later in the afternoon and I felt the urge to connect with Mum. When I dropped in, I saw Mum sitting watching the light. I looked at the light and saw that it had changed overnight. It was now spinning like a spiral vortex. Its rays were shining more vibrantly and it appeared to be spinning on its own axis point. As I watched the light spinning and moving faster, it was creating a vacuum sensation. I saw debris being pulled into the light. The voice spoke to me, "Everything is returning to source now. All particles which are the same are being collected." I could not take my eyes off the light as I watched it grow and intensify, yet at the same time it felt softer and gentle and I felt more connected to the light.

Mum suddenly stood up and walked towards my dad's family. She embraced them all and stood with them. I couldn't hear any words; it was once again inner communication. I felt their happiness and joy as they embraced. It felt as though they were reminiscing on their lives together. Mum began to walk to other family members of my dad's and walked past the light. She widened her step away from the light and stopped to look up at it. She made me laugh because she looked at the light then looked toward me and pulled a funny face and kept her distance. I was feeling and hearing everything from everyone; it was all being expressed into and through my body. I laughed at Mum because she was saying, "I'm not ready to go near that light yet." Mum looked behind her at her own family. She stood starring at them, then looked toward me and told me, "I'm not ready to go to them yet." I looked at her family and they were still there, patiently waiting, nothing had changed since they first appeared.

Still standing looking around, Mum asked, "Where's your Father?" I replied, "He is here." I looked towards where I felt Dad was. He was not form, I could see him moving toward us but he was not as a body. He appeared as energy, orbs of light moving toward us. I felt overwhelmed, my whole being felt electrified as the orbs of energy came closer. I cried as joy filled my heart. I felt my dad through my entire body; he was filling every particle of space inside me. I felt him, heard him and knew him in every cell of my being. There was no separation from myself to my dad. For the first time in my life I understood the meaning of we are one. I was sobbing uncontrollably, and voiced out loud to my sisters who were in the hospital room with me, "Oh my God this is incredible." As the lights and orbs came closer I heard Dad say, "Your mother's not ready to see me yet. I cannot appear until it is time and she is comfortable, that's why I am not appearing as form."

Mum came back over to where I was sitting and told me, "You all know what to do," (referring to my sisters and I) "don't get caught up in the little stuff. There is a lot more to come, don't prolong this, I'm alright." She was teary now as she looked at me. I felt a deep letting go and a sadness that went along with this. Mum said, "I'm alright, I know the doors have been closed now and we can't go back." I looked at Mum feeling a bit strange and said, "What! I'm going back." Mum smiled at me through her tears. I saw how easy it was for me to come and go as I was still attached to my body. While in this emotional state energy appeared behind Mum. It had no form, yet

I just knew it was there to support Mum while she dealt with the deeper emotions that were surfacing.

Another energy shift was happening and as I looked at Mum I could see the realisation on her face that she was not coming back. I could hear in my mind her thoughts; she was thinking of her home and her garden. She was worried about the mess that was left in her home after the window had to be broken to reach her.

I was calming Mum in my own way, when I saw the light behind Mum was also pouring light into her. The main source of light was intensifying in brightness as it began to change shape. The top of the light vortex began to spread out like a flat disk shape as it covered the entire top of the scene we were in. More images appeared behind Mum's family, they were not bodies, but silhouettes of people. Then more appeared, they were not recognisable, they were light bodies. Mum looked at me to see if I too saw them, I nodded in response. She asked me, "Are we dreaming?" I shook my head and told her this was really happening.

So much was happening I didn't know where to look. Suddenly Dad began to appear in form with orbs of light still surrounding him. I looked at Mum but she did not see him. The voice spoke to me, "Do not worry about the details now, and there is more to come." There were flashes of details moving through my mind now, and in my heart, I knew that somehow this was in preparation for the ending of mum's physical life. My sensory perception was in overdrive, everything my body felt was intensified, yet it appeared that I was the only one experiencing it to this degree.

The energy behind Mum began to glow differently and another shift in energy sent a huge surge throughout my body. Mum was relaxed and peaceful as she leaned in and placed her head on my shoulder. The relief I felt in my own body was incredible. Mum was peaceful now and resting. I opened my eyes and sister number three was still curled up with her head in the exact position as Mum. I asked her, "Did you feel that?" She did, and was also in awe of the energy and feelings in the room. We shared together the deep release we both had experienced within our own bodies. Looking at Mum lying in the hospital bed we could see and feel the changes in her body. She was breathing deeply as the letting go process was also happening to the body.

The cleaners arrived a few moments later and we sat and watched them tidy up the room and clean it thoroughly. When they left my sister and I laughed and told Mum, "See, you have your tidy room now." The room had been physically cleansed but it also felt as though a deep spiritual cleanse had occurred.

More family members arrived and my older sisters as well; we were all together now. It reminded me when we would all meet at Mum's house for our

Saturday morning coffee and chat, as someone was always arriving at the hospital room with cups of coffee.

Later that evening, Mum's breathing deteriorated. I felt the need to connect once more with Mum. I never said anything to my sisters and family members but I felt this would be the last time. I wrote everything down that happened and asked my niece to scribe for me anything I managed to say. I didn't want to break this final alignment with Mum.

This time connecting to Mum I felt her agitation as she said, "There's so much happening now. I'm still torn, so much has happened. Why does it have to be like this? I'm so torn!" Mum was emotional again. She was trying to focus on us sitting in the room with her. I was trying to calm her but she kept trying to turn her body around to go back. She cried, "I didn't mean for all of you to go through this. I didn't mean for this to happen, not like this." Each time Mum tried to turn back, her body in the hospital room became agitated and I could hear her moaning in the room; this was the first time there had been any movement or sound from her body in 24 hours.

In the space where Mum was, I placed my arms around her now to hold her tight and prevent her from turning back. This was her suffering now; trying to return to the body and not the peaceful place she was at. This was the hardest moment for me, to hear her moaning through the body and knowing that she was already in a state of leaving the body. She tried to go back three times before she settled.

Mum told me that the hardest part of this is having people do things for her; she doesn't like it when people do things for her and she can't give back to them. I reassured her that we were all here because we would not want to be anywhere else, this was our healing as we let go. I could feel Mum crying but it was a deep internal feeling as there were no physical tears appearing.

Energetically we moved towards where I saw Dad. He was shimmering and not quite in form. Mum stood and looked at everyone; she seemed to be scanning them all. They were also just standing looking at Mum. Then she looked at me and said, "I can see them all." With this recognition, Dad became clearer and Mum could now see him. I knew that this was the moment Dad had been waiting for before he could appear. Mum was standing between me and Dad now and kept looking back to me for reassurance.

The energy changed and a peaceful energy filled the space. I felt in my heart this was Mum's feeling when she finally saw Dad; it settled her agitation. Dad came forward and stood in front of mum. He placed his hands outwards for Mum to hold them. I thought she would rush into his arms but she hesitantly took his hands and now stood with him.

Still holding hands, Dad rubbed Mum's wedding ring finger and looked up at me. He did this about three times before I heard in my mind, "Your mother does not have her wedding ring on. Where is it?" They both stood together and it seemed as if time was standing still. There was no movement from either of them until Mum turned and looked at me, as if she was checking to see if I was still with her. Mum looked shy and her head was lowered. Then Dad spoke and told her, "It's alright" he took a step closer to Mum. Now standing right in front of her, he looked towards me and shrugged his shoulders as if to say he wasn't sure what else to do. Dad placed his arm around her and drew her close to him. As he did this he gently placed her head onto his chest and held her close. I felt a deepening presence, that of reassurance and support enter me. I then realised that this was what Dad was giving to Mum.

They stood like this for a few minutes, no movement just stillness. I saw Mum try and pull back from him, wanting to look behind her back to me. He held her firmly against his chest, not hard but gently holding her head, resting it on him. I began to feel cold. My entire body was shivering and shaking, inside and out. This was what Mum was feeling within her and I was feeling her energy. Dad looked towards me and just glared at me. I remembered at that moment thinking, there's the look, the look I remember from my childhood.

As I watched from a distance, Mum had settled

and felt at ease with Dad. She was starting to accept that she was here with Dad. Even though I watched them from a distance, I could feel my father's energy close to me. I heard him speak, that he was now ready to take her back to her family. I shared with Dad how I thought it was supposed to be my job to do this. He explained that he was the one who took her from her birth country and her ancestors therefore; it was his role to bring her home. While he was sharing all of this I did not notice Mum's family move closer and were now to my left. My grandmother, my mum's mother, was right by my side. She leaned against me and shared with me a deeper bond that I have come to associate with her and my mum's ancestors. I had felt this bond for many years and only now could I feel the sacredness of this whole experience.

As I turned back to my parents, they were walking toward us arm in arm. As they got closer I felt another shift in energy. I saw a very intense flame glowing as it appeared out of nowhere. I became extremely hot and very uncomfortable as this flame radiated heat. I heard, "Don't dilly dally. This is a slow process but not much time now" A smile came to my face at this comment, "Don't dilly dally." I had heard it many times through guidance when there was something that needed to be done.

The flame was quite intense, I could not focus properly. One thing I had noticed was Mum had not spoken since she stood with Dad.

The flame grew stronger as I began to see images of Dad when he was younger. Again, I found myself smiling at these images. I could feel him now in my energy field; he was so close to me, it was really strong. I heard him say, "Your mother will be alright." I was not able to move, I felt I needed to wait in this place with my grandmother. A peaceful and happy feeling moved into me.

My grandmother placed her arm around me and I heard, "Your deepest destiny is hidden in your deepest mind, only when you find this will you understand." I felt uneasy now and noticed my parents standing still, just waiting, everyone was waiting. What were they all waiting for? I felt a little overwhelmed by it all, and then Dad was at my right side. He hugged me, and wanted me to come closer to them both. I declined, not because I didn't miss him or love him but because I just knew I needed to observe and watch from a distance. From within the silhouettes of Mum's ancestors, there was movement. I saw a woman walk towards my mum and could hear the name Mina, "I am Mina. She is closest to me." I realised this was my great grandmother, my mum's grandmother.

Finally, Mum was responding and began to move and look upon her grandmother. She became emotional and I felt her energy once more. I asked Dad to help and reassure Mum as her grandmother held her for the first time since they were separated through death during the war.

Something had shifted in Mum as she now acknowledged her parents and her sister. She was smiling and crying, looking very happy as she walked through the crowd of ancestors holding her mother's hand. I looked for Dad and he was still beside Mum. Mum appeared very innocent, like a child, yet there was strength glowing from her as she walked with pride amongst her ancestors.

The flame had settled now that Mum had connected back to her family. I watched everyone turn toward the light. Strange images began to appear in my mind as I stood watching. These images were abstract triangular points and shapes. I could not make sense of them as they moved through my mind. Everyone except my parents slowly moved towards the light. There was no movement from Mum and Dad, they had stopped and were also watching everyone move closer to the light. As I stood a few metres away, more people were gathering. I could not make out a distinct image, just lots of movement towards the light.

Dad looked at me and I felt him wanting me to come closer. I shook my head; I did not want to go closer. Now Mum was looking at me and asked, "Why can't we all be here, everyone together?" Then I heard Dad share with her, "At first it seems like you leave, soon you will see the truth" As I listened to my dad I just knew deep down that something about this statement sat right at my very core. As I felt this deep inside me, the light intensified; it was shining so bright now. It was also growing with intensity and the energy beams radiating from it were beautiful. The beams of light energy began to wash over everyone, me included. I felt a deep peace as the energy waves moved through my body touching me deep inside. These feelings were amazing as the energy beams continued to bathe us with their light.

Without physically moving, I was now standing with my parents. I grabbed my mum's hand and giggled to myself as the waves of light increased and moved throughout my body. The heat returned and I could feel it on my face. It was so concentrated that it began to slightly push me and pulsate like a strong pressure on my body.

Images once more appeared in my mind, this time of Lion's heads. A tunnel appeared in my mind, spinning, and the Lion's heads moved into and through the tunnel. The images changed once they entered the tunnel. I was seeing old imagery of countries and people. It felt like the days of Jesus Christ, with similar dress and housing. Next, I saw shop windows flash by with different scenes in them ranging from the early 1900's to now. It all happened so fast, I could not make it all out. The tunnel began to slow down and finally disappeared. I noticed the scene with my parents and that the light had also stopped. It was strange as though we were locked in time.

Then my past began to move in my mind's eye,

childhood memories, and happy times with my friends and the neighbour's dog. Then more scenes from my past appeared. It was all so quick, nothing stayed long enough to take in. Something happened when I was looking at my past; my parents had moved away from me and were now close to the light. Clearly I heard the voice within say, "Time stands still. Things only get caught in time but healing cannot occur in time." I was shown how we get caught up in time and illusion and create a time warp, continually travelling into the same thoughts and projections. Relief came from this moment and I focused back on my parents.

There were people walking into the light and merging with it. Mum was happy now. She saw me standing near her and it felt like she was only seeing me for the first time and was surprised I was standing with her. For a moment, it felt she had forgotten where she was. I hugged her and Dad leaned in and gave me a big hug. In my mind, I heard him say, "You will be alright." A huge release surged through my body. I could hear Mum's breathing in the hospital room changing. She was breathing very shallow now. I looked upon my mum and told her how much I loved her. She shared with me how hard this was to leave us all behind. Then she laughed and asked me, "Is this all real? I can breathe properly here and I can walk properly here. There's no pain, I'm not nervous here." She continued to chuckle to herself as she noticed the difference in this place we were in.

An enormous surge of energy permeated from the light and then I understood it's not the light giving off this energy but the people returning to the light that caused it. As everyone disappeared into the light, it began to grow and I felt a profound stillness take over my body. I found it difficult to be present in the hospital room as my body was being pulled deep into the energy of the light. I was aware of my physical body slowing down and my head begin to droop forward. I could feel a part of me still in the room, yet with each dropping sensation deeper into my body I was unable to move at will. It felt like a deep meditation; so deep that the body and Soul were slowly separating, yet awareness was still present.

My sisters had become aware of the change in my body. I could hear them discussing with themselves if I was still there. They wanted to know if I was alright. I could hear them talking to me softly but I could not function in my body, I could not answer them. They became concerned now; one of them touched my hand to get a reaction. I wished I could just tell them how wonderful and peaceful I was. It took all my will power to connect back into the body, yet all I was able to say was, "I'm okay" in a gentle whisper. As soon as the words came out I was catapulted right back to the light and my parents standing in front of it. For a moment, I wondered if this was what it was like for Mum.

Everyone had now left except my parents; they had their backs to the light looking at me. They were peaceful and I was aware of Mum's breathing becoming even slower between each breath. Then my parents took a step together, back towards the light and I heard Mum take another breath in the hospital room, then nothing. I was consciously waiting for the next breath wondering if this would be her last, then another step back and another breath, then silence. Everything had slowed down including the length between breaths. It felt as though at any moment Mum would stop breathing.

During these last steps looking at my parents, I felt content and happy, and as I watched, Mum was smiling back at me. They stepped again and were directly in the centre of the light. I heard the breath in the room. Mum was still smiling at me and waved; she was glowing. I knew in my heart she was going. Then the light consumed them. They didn't go anywhere, they became light. I couldn't see them anymore; the physical image was gone. My heart expanded and opened and in this moment a profound relief and understanding moved through my body. I felt a sense of freedom. I was happy and I was smiling inside.

I heard my sisters crying in the room and realised that Mum had not taken another breath. She was gone from the body. I came back and opened my eyes, still with a glimmer of a smile, until my mind and the world I saw in front of me jolted me back to this reality and I cried with my sisters; my beautiful Mum was gone. My grief was full of sadness, yet the deep peace of my experience stayed with me. I cried as I held Mum; we all cried and grieved and held Mum. She looked beautiful in her death. She was peaceful. We noticed that she had dropped about thirty years in age, Mum looked younger. We all sat beside Mum for the next couple of hours as we talked, cried and laughed.

The next morning as I woke, I heard a song in my mind. All I could hear repeatedly was, "summer, winter, rain or fall, all you have to do is call and I'll be there, yes I'll be there." I woke up knowing that these songs are my inner messages and that all I had to do was call or tune into any one of the people who have died in my life and they will be there. I was feeling good but still had to get my head around everything that I had experienced over the last three days. I sat down to have my morning cup of tea when I felt the urge to write. I heard, *"There is so much to do, don't be disheartened by what you see or hear. Together all shall fall into place. Together love and laughter can flourish again, joining all as one as you heal parts of the past that have come between you all. Don't dismay as nothing unusual is occurring, nothing that is not the natural cycle of life. Devastation is only what each one makes of it. Devastation can be seen as rejuvenation but only when the mind shifts from attaching to letting go. As you attach you bring to you in this world more of what you are attaching to. When the mind lets go, a total union with self appears; judgements become the past and freedom becomes the now, then and only then, can happiness establish itself totally into each and every present situation."*

This experience confirmed deeply in my heart and mind, everything I have believed and experienced about physical death. My belief is the body dies yet the energy, the Soul that was in the body is always present. That it moves within and around us at every moment. The experience of feeling, hearing and seeing energy can be blocked based upon the individual's life and the upbringing they had. Each human being has a sensory perception that is more defined within them. Once the individual learns how to access their own senses they are more inclined to see, feel or hear.

I believe that there is nowhere to go and that all exists in this one moment. It is only the body that restricts us to the world of form, of solid matter. In and through the journey of death, the body's restrictions unlock as we transcend the body and move into the realm of spirit, of energy.

As we journey through life we often ask the Question why. Why are we here? Why would we want to come into a body? These questions cannot be answered by another person. They must be experienced individually. We all have a part of life within us, yet each part is different and seems separate to another's. It is through our differences that we learn about each other, and ultimately, we learn about life and death.

I can only share my experiences here and how my life through this body, came to understand another's life as they left the body. These experiences help me to go beyond what my mind interprets in the world. Beyond to a place that has touched my very core, my very existence, and this has nothing to do with the world I see. This place moved me beyond my body, my rational mind; it freed me from my own self limitations. Life now touches a note deep inside me, the place inside of me that holds my truth. The truth of who I really am based upon all my healed experiences so far.

CHAPTER 11

THE ULTIMATE TRUTH

There are many valid experiences and ways that Spirit connects with you, just know that patience and stillness can help the process.

CHAPTER 11

THE ULTIMATE TRUTH

Experiences in life can bring about fear and apprehension especially when there is a trigger that unlocks past emotional experiences. Certain times of the month, year and even seasons can bring forth memories that had never left. These memories are hidden and safely tucked away in the deepest parts of the unconscious mind. When they are opened and looked at again, the same emotion rises, yet it gets easier to deal with each time.

So here I am once again in winter and the month of June with nothing unusual happening except for the nagging feeling and constant pressure from guidance to contact sister number 3. I kept hearing her name in my mind and the voice telling me to ring her. I did not feel any distress over this message, so I put it off until one evening the feeling inside of me became unbearable as I heard again, "Ring your sister"

Finally, I made the call and my brother-in-law answered. I asked to speak to my sister and he handed her the phone. When I heard her voice, I began to feel uneasy. I shared with her that I have felt the need to contact her for the past few days now and asked if everything was alright. She told me that she also wanted to talk to me and had been thinking about me. She then shared that there was something going on with her health and she needed more tests tomorrow. I asked, "What sort of tests, what's happening?" She told me that they had found a growth in her abdomen.

I felt as though my whole body had skipped a beat. Did I hear right, did she say growth? I started to shake and felt ill but continued to listen to my sister share this news with me. Even though I was scared I could feel a calmness coming from my sister. She was in control, calm and factual. Then my brother-in-law came back on the phone and shared how they didn't want anyone to know until they had more results. He told me that just before I rang, they had spoken about not ringing me until they knew more. We both laughed as I blatantly told him, "Did you really think you could keep something like this from me?"

The next day was a very long day waiting for the phone to ring. I was still trying to process this information as I hoped and prayed for the best positive outcome. I prayed that she would be alright. I was trying to be strong but the truth was I was scared. I was scared for my sister as we were very close, not just in age but in sisterly connections.

It was late that evening when I got the phone call. The tests were back and they were not looking good. They showed the growth had metastasized and travelled to other organs in her body. As we talked I could feel the shift in her voice, even though she sounded calm she was also worried. I was trying to be supportive and positive, sharing with her that these types of things can be healed and she would be alright. At the time, I truly believed that she would be, that my sister would survive. I needed to believe this not just for her but for myself. I was scared and fearful and could not imagine what it would be like for her to have this diagnosis.

It began to feel surreal, this cannot be happening, it's not right. This was where my thoughts were going with all this information. How could someone be working one day, feel sick the next and nearly collapse the day after?

It had been a day now since my conversation with my sister. I knew that trust was needed here, not just any trust but trust for something greater than me was needed. I dealt with this as I do any emotional state in my life; I meditated. I surrendered my fears, my thoughts and my prayers deeply into the meditation.

Throughout the day, I felt the need to contact her again but kept putting it off. Not knowing how she was and trying to settle myself was difficult. I began to feel a stronger pull to contact her as I now recognised the sensation of energy surging inside me. My energy vibrates inside me when guidance is pushing me to do something. I finally dialled her number and she was resting in bed. She was feeling unwell and very weak. I asked her to call someone who could help her, who could come and see her. Her answer was, "No, I'm alright." I knew deep inside that she was not alright. I asked her to go to the hospital but again she pushed that away. Eventually after much persuasion she promised that when her husband came home she would go to the doctor or the hospital.

The very next day she was admitted to hospital and her journey began. A journey that seemed to last forever but in truth was very short. After a few days, it was obvious that things were changing very dramatically for her. Test results revealed more tumours were found. It was at this moment I knew I had to be with her, so I booked a flight and flew home the next day.

The anxiety in my body was extreme as I packed my clothes and prepared myself to help my sister in any way I could. I was trying not to think too much as I was frightened for her. My blood pressure was high so I went to the doctor before getting on the plane and was prescribed blood pressure medication. Within eight hours of taking the medication I noticed a rash appear on my chest and arms. I knew it was from the medication, and then I heard the voice within, "You do not need to take this medication. Your heightened pressure is only a symptom of stress and will subside as the issue subsides." I stopped taking the medication, trusting in my guidance and knowing that I am an anxious person in these circumstances and this too shall pass.

Arriving at the hospital was like a déjà vu of the arrival at hospital when Mum had the stroke. As I walked into the room I saw family members around her and it was then I felt a sigh internally and my inner pressure subsided. It was enough for me to be with my sister, my family and talk to her.

She opened her eyes when she heard my voice and smiled at me. She was tired and on medication but she was also in good spirits. I watched her each time she opened her eyes as she was present with whoever was visiting her or talking with her. Then she would close her eyes and I saw her energetically drop deeply into herself once more.

There was so much positive energy in the room as each person bought into the room a part of themselves and their connection to her. She was strong and always made an effort to open her eyes and smile at everyone who was visiting. I knew that she was still listening to everyone even when her eyes were closed. My other two sisters and I would sit around her bed, laughing and saying funny jokes and moments in our days. It was then my sister lying there would smile and shake her head at the three of us. She was listening but was too weak to interact.

There were times when I was alone with my sister. I would sit by her side and place my hands on her body and drop deeply within to meditate. While in meditation, I would recite my Mantra, a verse for spiritual healing. I was deep in meditation when I felt a shift in energy. I opened my eyes and my sister was looking at me, smiling. I looked at her and laughed and said, "Sprung" and asked her if she heard me. She smiled and said, "Yes." These were precious moments for me as I knew she was peaceful inside and resting.

The vigilance continued at her bedside. Everyone continued to bring energy to the room that only family and friends could understand because they all knew her. They knew the beautiful angelic person that she was, a gentle peaceful person who we all knew. I was very positive not wanting to listen to the doctors when they told the family she only had a week to live. I could not take that information in, it was not true. I was in shock, the doctors were wrong. A week ago, she was working, running her business and just feeling a bit off. There must be something they could do.

I prayed, I meditated, I did everything I knew spiritually to do, yet she was still slipping away slowly each day. The doctors talked about a cure for the form of Melanoma she had and they began a treatment that day. This bought a high vibe and energy back to the room. I wanted to stay and help her through this. I asked all my colleagues and friends in the healing circles to help heal my sister. I began to meditate deeper, asking for support and guidance and staying with her as long as I could each day.

The new medication was difficult for the staff to administer as my sister was weaker now and had difficulty swallowing. I was asked to go into the room and help with support. I placed my hand on her back and rubbed her stomach as she tried to swallow the tablet. Her eyes were wide open as she looked at me. I saw for the first time a spark of my sister wanting to try, wanting to heal herself, yet at the same time through her eyes I heard her say, "Thank you for helping me, I will be alright." When I heard this I felt relieved, I felt that this was it, she will come back from this. How wrong was I because this was the last time I saw my sister alive.

I left the hospital after she had taken the medication feeling the need to rest and have a good night's sleep. Back at my oldest sister's home we both settled down and talked about the day's events. We knew it was getting close to her next dose of medication and we both kept a close eye on the clock. At 10.20pm we looked at each other knowing that the next dose was administered, yet we both felt uneasy. We were worried that she was not strong enough to swallow the tablets. My oldest sister was very agitated; she was so worried about our sister. Then the phone rang and we both jumped and looked at each other. My heart was racing as my sister answered the phone. I heard her say, "Okay, what happened?" She kept repeating, "What happened?" She hung up the phone, looked at me and said, "We have to get to the hospital she has had a turn." We didn't really know what had happened; we just knew she has had a turn.

We are both strong women, yet this night the shock and fear came rushing into both of us. Internally I was shaking; my body had gone into shock. I began to recognise this feeling of anxiety when there has been tragedy in the past. When shock enters my body, I also notice an inner strength enter, a strength that propels me to rise above the fear. I tried not to allow my fear to take hold as we really didn't know the outcome. On the way to the hospital, we picked up our other sister and travelled together to the hospital.

There was so much happening energetically in the car that we all went into our own way of dealing with the crisis. My oldest sister was not coping and found herself in the midst of anxiety. I was in the back shaking inside, when I saw in my minds eye my dad. He said, "Your sister is with me now. She is alright."

I did not want to believe this, maybe it was my imagination, maybe she was alright and still with us. I had been doing the Emotional Freedom Technique (EFT) to help me cope with the intensity of emotions flowing through my body. Even after my experience with my dad I was still in shock as we entered the hospital.

Upon arriving, we were told she had died after the last dose of tablets. Her heart was weak and stopped beating. She was gone. As we entered the room it felt unreal, my sister laying there, my niece holding her crying. My sisters and I just stood looking at this scene until the first tear fell and one by one we began to cry and grieve for our sister.

As my tears fell I was aware of my sister's voice in my mind. I could hear her trying to speak to me. I wasn't listening as I was still in shock, until I heard her clearly say, "Tell them I am here." She was repeating this over and over in my mind. I knew in my heart it was her. I had to push this away, I couldn't say it. Everyone was in grief, crying and trying to deal with what was in front of them and that the reality was she was gone from her body. I found this difficult to deal with personally and I am the one who believes and feels this truth. I had to tell her to stop, "I can't, not yet it's not right."

After a couple of hours, the family were still together beside her, talking and sharing and saying our goodbyes. My nephew was standing over his mum allowing his tears to fall, when I heard my sister once more, "Tell them I'm here." This time when I heard her speak to me I felt connected to her enough to share as I trusted in the right moment. I addressed everyone and told them, "Since I entered the room she has wanted me to tell you all she is still here in the room." At that moment, the drawer on the bedside table flew open and hit my nephew in the leg. He jumped and looked at me and I laughed and said out loud, "I told you she was here." She had made her presence felt just as I had spoken the words. We all laughed together as the connection between the two worlds appeared.

For me it was a confirmation of the life I live and the beliefs I have due to many experiences with life after death. You would think that my experiences would lessen the emotional grief but no, it is always the same. You must go through the emotions to come out the other side. It is only then, that you can begin a process of change as you understand the gifts that each experience brings into your reality.

Throughout my experiences with those who have passed, the first few days after their passing has the strongest connection this begins to fade over time. As time goes by, the Soul calms and begins its own internal journey of acceptance and understanding. This can take a few months as the Soul adjusts into the understanding of not having a physical body. With my sister, it was so real, and seemed easy for her to connect.

The next day I was in the bathroom doing my morning ritual of cleansing and moisturising, when I heard my sister's voice once again in my mind, "Are you still using that same moisturiser?" I laughed out loud as I heard this because when we were younger we both would use the same moisturiser.

The communication began quickly and easily with my "Big Sis". She seemed very composed and inquisitive even though she had only been gone for 24 hours. Many times, I have questioned my connection to Spirit and many times I have been given proof that they are there as they find different ways to communicate. These moments give me reassurance and peace as I trust in these experiences instead of trying to push them away.

I cannot deny the connection and the gifts that are within me. These gifts help me at times like this and show me something greater than the human experience. These moments are felt and heard deep within me. Sometimes they are difficult to distinguish from my own inner thoughts or those that are placed into me from Spirit. Not everyone will have this connection to Spirit, yet I do believe that everyone has a deep connection to the universal source energy. It is through our awareness of spiritual connections and energy fields that we can find our own unique gift in and through the embodiment of the Soul.

The days after her passing were slow, difficult and emotional as we were trying to come to an understanding of what had happened. For me, I was ready to apply all my knowledge, experience and healing to help my sister. To help her heal, stay and live longer was my goal, yet after the first few days it became apparent to me that this was not going to happen. This was when I felt the emotion of being helpless and feeling deep anxiety, watching the spiral of life being taken from someone dear to me. It was my sister's strength and gentle conviction that kept me from falling apart in front of her.

The next morning, I woke hearing my name being called three times. It was loud and echoed in my room. I opened my eyes and expected to see my sister standing there. I heard her voice and knew it was her calling my name. She would use this tone in her voice as she called to me in life as well. Lying there, I listened and waited, I could feel her presence in the room; I knew she was there. Then nothing as though a door had been closed.

Throughout the day, I began to experience movement in my peripheral vision. I would notice this movement to my side and quickly look; expecting to see something or somebody, but once my eyes focused, nothing was there. I understand now after many years of this occurring and not just when people crossover, that Spirit is close but the veil between the two worlds is still dense so we cannot focus through the body's eyes. There are some who have the gift of clairvoyance, clear seeing in this reality. My gifts are internal and as a child I asked for them to stop appearing outside of me as it would scare me back then.

Later that day I experienced a nudge in my lower back as I was standing lighting incense. It was as though somebody placed their hand onto my lumbar region and pushed hard; hard enough that I jolted forward. Instantly I asked the question "Who was that?" and saw my sister in my mind's eye. Over the many years of experiencing energy and Spirit connections, I receive an answer to a question sometimes even before I have finished asking. I have learnt to trust this form of communication and the instant image or answer I receive, which was not easy in the beginning. My mind would doubt and question what I was receiving. Eventually I accepted that this was guidance and it was always consistent. It never changed in the form it came; it was only my mind that tried to change it.

Knowing and feeling her presence did not change what I was experiencing. I was shaken and going through the emotions every day. She was gone, yet she was still present. My mind, my heart, my whole being was still trying to piece it all together. This time, I was not able to justify or take the emotion into my spirituality. I began to question everything about life and death, and the why's and how's. I began to ask my sister to give me something that I could use in the world to help me take this experience deeper to understand it.

I wanted the biggest epiphany I have ever had regarding death. I was writing my book, this book that seems to have its own story. One that weaves its path throughout the pages, with stories of deep and emotional experiences "Where will it end?" I thought. When I first spoke to my sister regarding her health I had a thought and a flash of energy in my heart. Something inside me was triggered. Later that day I thought to myself, "Please don't tell me my book will end with another death." The book began through death and it may end with death and here I am on the final chapter of this book. Many years have passed as I slowly digest, heal, and understand each and every one of life's experiences and life's endings.

I am hoping by the time I have finished this chapter it will all make sense, or it may all seem too emotional, futile and worthless. The experience with my sister was the deepest and strangest experience I have faced through death. There is a part of me that feels disconnected and separate from the whole encounter, yet deep within something has opened and is beginning to flow into my life.

Many people came to say goodbye and to celebrate her life. The day became a blur as I sat with close friends and family members. Then something strange caught my gaze. I noticed a beautiful dove sitting on the fence. Now many of you may say that's not strange but it was as we were at a family member's place who owns a lot of cats; Birds knew better than to sit in close proximity of the house. The dove kept drawing my attention away from the crowd, until suddenly the bird flew under the veranda where over a hundred people were standing and sitting. The dove flew directly to my niece, whose mother had just passed. It circled above her head before it landed at her feet and looked up at her, chirping and singing as though it was communicating with her. I watched as the dove then flew over the crowd and flew around my sister's best friend who was with her when she passed. Finally, the dove flew out of the veranda and sat back on the fence. I looked over to my niece who was calling to me, in awe of what had just happened. We both knew at that moment, we had experienced my sister, her mum, in the form of a bird. This was a beautiful moment in an already emotional day.

In life, we don't choose to delve into and understand death; we try not to think about it. For some this can be very traumatic, not just thinking about their own mortality but the mortality of those you love.

Children and young adults are seldom witness to the experience called death. The topic is shunned and they are told little about the experience, yet in life it is one of the many consistent experiences that we face as a human being. It's like anything really, if you have never heard about it or have not learned about it, then you will feel vulnerable, fearful and inadequate around it. It is only through consistency that we learn to adjust and accept deeper emotional experiences.

In all the experiences so far, does death become easier? Not yet, and I don't want the experience to be easier. What I really want and need from these experiences is closure but ultimately an understanding that life and death in all stages can bring me grief. It is the way I deal with the stages that holds the emotions within me. My spiritual connection to God, to source, to the voice within, helps me to cope, feel and accept what is. In the beginning the human "will" wants to know that loved ones are still present. Sometimes this can cloud the experience of gentle healing waves that naturally encompass you through the first stages of grief.

Many people ask why? Why can't I connect? Why can't I hear? Why can't I feel them? My answer to this is to stop. Stop and drop inside you. Make time in your day to rest, connect and wait. Be assured they are close, even closer straight after death. Practice mindfulness, clearing your mind and don't have any expectation of how this will happen. Everyone will experience these contacts differently. My personal connections with Spirit were all so different, they can appear through your own thoughts and inner voice, as spirit outside of you, synchronistic signs, messages, nature, insects, animal kingdom and even dreams.

One of the more tangible experiences can come through dreams. The night my sister passed, my aunt had a dream. In the dream her husband woke her from sleep saying to her, "Your brother is on the phone." Her brother, my father, was in spirit and had passed years before. She was annoyed at his comment and in the dream told him, "Don't be silly he's dead, it can't be him." Her husband was persistent and handed her the phone. The phone was glowing green and vibrating. She placed the phone to her ear and her brother's voice clearly spoke to her. He said, "She is with me now, everything is alright." When my aunt woke the next morning, she was told the news that her niece had passed away through the night.

These are the messages from Spirit that give more proof that life and death are but one continuum. We are still connected energetically to the soul of the person who was once in a body, and how they interact with us and how we interact with them is an individual thing. If your mind is open and you don't have any expectations on how or when contact will happen, it can be seen in numerous forms and experiences.

After personal death and tragedy, some are looking for signs that their loved ones are present. It is within the first four to six weeks that the connection is strongest, before it begins to fade slightly as the Soul reaches an acceptance. The energy becomes subtle and easier to connect to through a mind and heart that is clear and beginning to heal. Sometimes a search begins outside of you, to find a message in life, in nature or even a touch of your hair. There are many valid experiences and ways that Spirit connects with you, just know that patience and stillness can help the process.

My personal experiences of death, dying and

passing have given me a deeper understanding of when and how contact is made. Realising that the how, when and where the contact is made is out of my control. Now I am settled internally once more, allowing myself to relax and drop into me through meditation. When and if anyone wishes to be present and contact me through signs or messages, I am open enough and clear in mind to piece the jigsaw together.

My niece was given a beautiful message days after the funeral. She was in a gift store filling in time on her lunch break when she turned to see a sign; tangible and literally in front of her. The wooden sign had her name and her mother's name written on it. The names were side by side, one name was written in block letters and the other was written in cursive. She looked in disbelief, not at the names but the way they were written. In their family business, her mum would always write their names in the day book in the exact same way. She was so overwhelmed and full of goosebumps at the names in front of her that she took a photo on her phone to look back on.

These moments are signs and messages formed in this reality not just by you through energy, but also by Spirit. These signs occur in the reality of the believer with an open and inquisitive mind. The energy field can expand as the mind opens to other possibilities and probabilities. When there is doubt, lack of trust or fear in the mind, Spirit cannot transform what we believe is solid, into new images and forms in the world.

The deeper messages I received came daily. They were sometimes subtle, yet always inspiring. Arriving back home after the funeral, I was in a different place emotionally. When I say different, I mean I was not sure what had just occurred over the last couple of weeks. It seemed a blur and surreal. I did not want to spiritualise my sisters passing; I wanted to feel every part of the grief and the emotion. I tried so hard to not want a sign or a message but that was not going to happen. My sister's energy was so close, I could not deny this. Random things began to happen when I settled back into me and my life. I began to experience shadows out of the corner of my eye, yet when I turned to look there was nothing or no one there. Then one evening relaxing in the lounge room I kept seeing someone standing near my hallway. I brushed it off because I knew that if I tried to see, it wouldn't be there. The energy was persistent and I began to feel them as a part of my awareness was gently being pulled towards them. About thirty minutes later I walked down the hallway to the bathroom. It was there that I heard my sister's voice so clear, "That was funny, you just walked straight through me." I laughed out loud as I could hear her laughing with me. These are the moments that make my heart sing. I don't feel sad at these times, I feel uplifted and with a sensation of deep clarity and acceptance.

Unravelling is the only way to explain my experiences and the last experience with my sister felt different. When I say the last I do not mean the last time this will happen. I am quite aware that over time this will happen again and again. Where I am now in my life based on choices and experiences in my own life is the need to not have her in my mind at every moment. Right now, I do not feel the need to see her, feel her or hear her. What I am aware of are my emotions and when they rise and fall. Allowing them to come to a peak and go with them instead of trying to justify them with my beliefs and spiritual sensitivities. When I feel her, I talk to her and when I see her photo I smile at her and say, "Hello." This time around I am gentle with me and try to keep a balance in my life. My balance is part physical, with living and working and part spiritual meditation with deep connection to me, plus many moments of Spirit contact. This is my perfect balance and it works for me. Even now, I still feel the pain when I reminisce about her and sometimes cry when I talk about her especially to family members. These moments are natural and quite normal to have for many months, years and even forever.

Even with these moments, the deepest core of me is peaceful. Peaceful about everything that has happened in my life and I feel all of them in my heart as the pain is transformed into an understanding. I now understand they are not accessible in this life in a body, yet are in spirit. The death of the Soul is the illusion.

I have looked at these experiences from many angles and in many different conversations with colleagues, friends and family. The one truth that always appears to me through these experiences is the body has ended its cycle and yet Soul is still present in this reality. Through energy, communication is still possible although it is not constant. It comes and goes and is transformed through the individual's sensory perception. They are close when I need guidance or just a nudge, or when they need to show or tell me something. They will find a way to get through.

It is through times of great sadness and grief that clarity and deepening of my understanding of life and death evolve. This clarity enables me to understand that life and death are but one continuum in this timeline. It also shows me that my mind, conscious or unconscious, can create in this reality. The idea of life and death being separate and "one" being the ultimate ending, changes as my views and feelings are changed through each individual experience.

Through the mind, we are attached to the form of the body and it is the mind that tells you that one day you will die. What the mind doesn't show you is that you are not the body; you are the Soul inside the body which is still connected to its true source and power. It is through our belief systems that we disconnect from source and connect to one individualised body. Only when you begin the process of connecting back to that which you really are, will you open to the worlds of energy, Spirit and source.

While in the body, you cannot fully experience the point of return from physical death. Those who have had near death experiences have been close and felt the connection to the truth, yet they have still been attached to the body to start again.

The closer one gets to death the more peaceful one becomes. Herein lays the indication but not the final experience. Until we truly leave the body, we cannot know beyond what we have heard, read, or experienced because we are still in a body. Sharing my personal experiences helps me to see beyond the tragedy that death brings. Each experience drops into me and somehow becomes a part of my journey here in the body.

Over many years, I have been asked on numerous occasions, "How can I hear Spirit? How can I see Spirit? And how can I feel Spirit?" The only way to begin this process if it is not a natural gift for you, is to have a clear and calm mind. There are different ways to clear and calm the mind but I can only share my experience and that is through mindfulness practice. If I begin my day with meditation, my mind is calmer and more receptive to subtle forms of energy waves and experiences.

After meditating one morning, I went out onto

my balcony to water my plants when a beautiful butterfly appeared. The butterfly flew past my face ever so gently as it continued around me and so close to me. The beauty of the butterfly made me stop what I was doing. I just watched it and noticed that it was different than the usual butterflies that meander over my balcony. The difference was its colouring; it was black with round circles of soft lavender all over it. I was mesmerised by this butterfly as I placed my hand out to touch it. The experience only lasted a few moments and then it was gone. I ventured downstairs to hang my washing out when the butterfly returned and once again flew around me and landed very close to me. Sitting on a blade of grass gently moving its wings, I began to feel the butterfly looking at me. It felt strange as though the butterfly was deliberately trying to get my attention. After a few minutes, I went upstairs to continue watering my plants when the butterfly was once again upstairs with me. I felt myself smiling inside and conversing with the butterfly, telling it how beautiful it was and thanking it for this experience. Then deep within I felt a shift as though something had just touched my core, my Soul. It was then I knew without a doubt that this butterfly represented my sister. There was no reason to this message and it certainly did not mean that my sister was now a butterfly. What I do believe is everything is energy, and that energy is always present and not just in the tangible presence of solid objects. If you understand that energy can never be destroyed and transforms itself into matter and molecules, then this is my understanding of my experience; energy that is still present from those who have been in a body can transform and create into form, or as we understand them to be, synchronistic events.

I began to understand that my sister is not separate from life. Her energy is still present as it deposits the subtle energy forms wherever and whenever needed. Energy transforms itself so it can be experienced through a body.

For those of us still in a body, this seems unimaginable. How can we be that free? How can we be everywhere at once? The answers do not fit into the mind's ideals of the body, or the struggles that are given through life in a body. Limitations are felt every day through the body. Constantly in our day to day activities we are faced with subtle limitations. They can be as simple as experiencing the body becoming tight as we age and not as flexible as we used to be. Or we may want to achieve a certain outcome in business, social, or pleasure that just doesn't happen. There are many varied limitations and some of you reading this would disagree, you may find that life is kind to you that your body is free and flexible. If you look into other areas of your life you may find that limitations occur in subtle energy forms, you may find it difficult to meditate or to understand how certain people live their lives.

These are all limitations based upon the soul being in the body/mind connection.

Throughout my journey, my home and the energy of the home has been an important factor. Many years ago when I began meditation, I noticed the room that was used for meditation had a certain vibe, a different lighter energy. This energy sustained itself and eventually permeated into the rest of the home. The source of this energy was the meditation room and healing space. People often commented on the peace they felt on entering my home. I began to move around a lot from house to house. It did not take me long to realise that the energy came with me as I set up each space, each altar and each room. My things, my ornaments, everything was imbued with this energy. When I packed, I would honour them and when I unpacked I would ask within where they would like to be placed. I would see a vision in my mind and intuitively hear and feel in my heart where and how each space would be set. This became second nature for me. I never questioned this communication with objects that did not appear to have life force energy.

Sitting in these sacred spaces within my home, I would notice a sound in the atmosphere. This sound was a hum that is perfectly aligned and balanced in the atmosphere. It took me a few years to realise that it was not the hum and peace of my home that was making me peaceful; it was the silence and stillness within me that was creating the external silence and peace outside of me. Now I get it, "You take yourself with you wherever you go."

There are times that the world affects my inner peace and I may feel imbalanced and emotional at times. The deep understanding of how to align myself gives me an advantage over the ups and downs of life.

It was four months after my sister's passing that she helped me understand the connection between energy spaces and Spiritual energy. It began in my upstairs bedroom when my husband and I were talking and making the bed. Before my sister passed, my husband and my sister had a standing joke between them. My sister would stir him up and say to him, "It's not all about you" as my husband has a very strong personality. Well this day he was stirring me and he spoke those words to me, "it's not all about you" and I replied, "It's not all about you" and we both laughed. It was at that moment a smoke alarm in my downstairs healing room began to go off. I ran downstairs thinking to myself, "I hope I blew out the candles earlier." My heart was racing as I ran down the back stairs. I opened the door expecting to see smoke but as I stepped inside, the alarm immediately stopped. I stood there shaking and confused. Then I felt her and heard her in my mind; it was my sister. I began to laugh out loud and asked if this was her setting off the alarm. She replied, "Yep that was me." I asked her why she set off the one downstairs and not upstairs where we were. She said, "It's easier for me to come through in this space." I knew she was talking about the energy, as downstairs was where I did all my work as an Intuitive therapist, including meditation groups. The message she shared that day was the importance of setting energy vibrations which are attuned to a particular frequency in the world of form. This frequency allows easy access for Spirit and Spiritual guidance to move into and through.

As I sit and contemplate death, all the experiences and so much more, I find myself smiling gently on the inside and sometimes on the outside. When I hear about friends and relatives who are grieving because of some form of loss, my own moments of grief show themselves in feelings of sadness and remembrance.

Over the years as a Holistic Counsellor and Intuitive therapist, I have experienced and now understand that emotions are energy caught up in a role play with us. It is through allowing the emotion to have its original experience without re-traumatising, that it begins the process of clearing. When you hold onto, block or push down emotions you are locking them into the emotional energy field of the human body. Releasing this energy out of the system brings peace, clarity of mind, and in some cases physical healing.

As my grieving process opens me to feel lighter, different and calmer, I can look back over not just my sister's death but all the heartaches of life and feel a truth beginning to touch the very core existence of who I am. I have learnt over the years to allow each experience to have its fullest moment; not denying or trying to change any of them. Finding my inner support team first as I meditate and surrender within, allowing myself to find moments of peace amongst the chaos of grief. Then finding support outside of me, in the world, through family, friends, colleagues and whichever direction I am pulled to look at. Eventually you come through the waves of emotion. You reach the other side of the grief and you sit watching and waiting for life to show you the next step, the next stage of your life. There is a truth showing itself to you, a truth that is always present in everything you do. Each individual will have their own truth that is created from the grief. This truth is not absolute, this truth is changeable just as this world changes because of grief.

Truth becomes a personal journey as each individual Soul has their own script to create and experience. While grief is present you may not be able to understand the dynamics of life and death.

My understanding of my journey is clear and my purpose is to heal my mind, my beliefs, and my grievances. I now truly understand it when I say, "I am not my body trying to find spirituality, and I already am a Spiritual energy trying to understand the human experience through a body."

ABOUT THE AUTHOR

CAROLINE BYRD IS THE OWNER OF SOULBYRDS: She is an author, speaker, seminar leader, developer of "Therapy for your Soul" and the founder of the breath of life meditation process. As an Intuitive therapist, with a diploma in holistic counselling, she has guided thousands of clients worldwide. Caroline has a rare talent of bridging the gap between the conscious and unconscious, the known and unknown using alternative healing modalities. Individuals and groups experience profound healing, awareness and insight as their consciousness expands to encompass a deeper perception of truth. Developing her natural gifts as an emotional intuitive, clairvoyant, psychic/medium, and spiritual channel, she uses her abilities to see beyond the body, the mind and its constraints, gently utilising her life skills, connection to spirit and training to go beyond the perceived world. All this, including her unique training through eastern meditation practices using the breath, make her a powerful and authentic, "Modern Therapist".

Caroline lives in Brisbane Australia where she has run her private practice for over 10 years. Her love of nature and the outdoors helps to ground the spiritual energy that flows through her as she walks amongst the trees and birds. Caroline's meditation practice is her Holy Grail where she communicates with guidance and is given insights not only into her life, but the life of humanity as a collective consciousness.

Connect With Caroline:

www.soulbyrds.com

Printed in the United States
By Bookmasters